THE NATURE AND EXTENT OF GOD'S KNOWLEDGE

DR. ROBERT A. MOREY

CHRISTIAN SCHOLAR S PRESS

The Nature and Extent of God's Knowledge

Robert A. Morey
Faith Defenders
P. O. Box 7447
Orange CA 92863

Printed in the United States of America

Scripture is taken from The Holy Bible, International Standard Version. Used by permission.

ISBN 1-931230-09-9
Library of Congress Catalog Card Number: [pending]

TABLE OF CONTENTS

INTRODUCTION

It is amazing that one would have to defend the Omniscience of God seeing it is enshrined in every major creed of Christianity since the first century. That the God of the Bible knows everything and that "everything" means EVERYTHING seems to be self-evident. But today the doctrine of God's knowledge has been once again cast into controversy.

This controversy is not some "ivory tower" issue such as counting the number of angels that can dance on the top of a pin. The Christian's confidence in the future turning out as God promised is the basis of the inspiration of Scripture, the sufficiency of the atonement and our hope of heaven.

The issue boils down to whether God controls the future or does the future control God? Does God's will determine what man does or does what man does determine God's will? Does God respond to man's decisions or does man respond to God's decisions? Do God's decrees precede or follow man's actions? Who acts first and who follows? Is God a knee-jerk deity?

The basis of our salvation and hope of heaven rests on the biblical and historic Christian view that God is infinite in His knowledge. There is simply no place in the universe where we can draw a line in the sand and say that God's knowledge starts or ends there. There is no hiding place to escape the omniscient eye of the Maker of heaven and earth.

PART I

PRINCIPLES OF APPROACH

As we begin our study of the nature and extent of the knowledge of God, we must emphasize that we are not referring to our knowledge of God. Instead, we are referring to God's knowledge of Himself and the universe He created. Does God know everything or are there some things which God cannot know?

It is thus very important that anyone who is going to discuss this issue "come clean" about the presuppositions he is bringing to the discussion. The failure to reveal the hidden principles that contextualize theological issues results in much confusion and self-contradiction. For this reason, we are going to lay out the principles that will guide us in our study of the nature and extent of the knowledge of God. To make them absolutely clear, we will contrast our principles with those of humanistic-based theologies.

The Christian View	The Humanistic Views
God's self-disclosure in Holy Scripture is the only way we can have true knowledge of the nature and extent of God's knowledge (1 Cor. 1:18-2:16).	Autonomous human reason unaided by divine revelation can discover the nature and extent of God's knowledge.
Thus the nature and extent of God's knowledge is the sole domain of special revelation and must be decided by Scripture alone (sola scriptura: 1 Cor. 4:6).	Thus the nature and extent of God's knowledge is not the sole domain of special revelation.

The Christian View	The Humanistic Views
The only method by which we can ascertain the teaching of Scripture on God's knowledge is the historical, grammatical, exegesis of relevant texts.	Philosophic reflection and argumentation is just as valid as biblical exegesis.
We must distinguish between primary and secondary texts. • "Primary texts" are those passages that have the nature and extent of God's knowledge directly in view. • "Secondary texts" are those passages that do not have God's knowledge in direct view but may by inference bear on the subject. Secondary texts must be interpreted in the light of the teaching found in the primary texts. Secondary texts cannot negate, overthrow or contradict the teaching found in primary texts.	There is no need to resort to such distinctions. Secondary texts are just as valid for proof texting as are primary texts.
The speculations of philosophy (Christian or pagan) that either contradict or go beyond the teaching of the primary biblical texts must be rejected as spurious. "Let God be true and every man a liar" (Rom. 3:4).	The speculations of philosophy (Christian or pagan) may modify or reject any aspect of divine revelation that is not in conformity to the opinions of the great philosophers.
Humanistic philosophy is built on the false doctrine of the autonomy of human reason. Scripture tells us that this is why philosophy never found God (1 Cor. 1:21).	If man is truly free, then he must not be limited by or to divine revelation. Man's autonomous reason is sufficient to discover the nature and extent of God's knowledge.

The Christian View	The Humanistic Views
The incomprehensibility of God means that we will not be able to explain fully the "whys" and "hows" of the divine revelation of the nature and extent of the knowledge of God.	We can modify or reject any aspect of the nature and extent of God's knowledge that we cannot fully explain. If we cannot explain "how" God can know something, then we can deny that he knows it.

The chart above reveals the presuppositions that guide most discussions of God's knowledge. If one begins with the assumption of human autonomy; i.e., that man can by reason alone determine what God can or cannot know, then he will eventually end up reducing God to what *man* can or cannot know. In effect, he ends up making a god in his own image.

On the other hand, if we begin with God's self-disclosure in Scripture, then we can have the certitude of absolute truth. Does this mean that we will be able to explain fully to everyone's satisfaction "how" God can know such things as the future? No. But this does not bother us in the least because faith swims when reason can no longer touch the bottom.

If Scripture is the revelation of an Infinite Mind and man has a finite intellect, then the finite mind of man will not be capable of an infinite understanding of what is revealed. This is why Scripture tells us that many of the truths it reveals go beyond the finite capacity of the human mind (Rom. 11:13; Eph. 3:19; Phil. 4:7; etc.). Is our appeal to the incomprehensibility of God a "cop out" as some humanistic theologians such as Clark Pinnock has charged? No. The doctrine of the incomprehensibility of God is the clear teaching of Scripture and we have yet to see any humanistic theologian even attempt to refute the exegetical evidence for it.[1]

Those who reject revealed truth because it does not "make sense" to them eventually end up in some form of atheism. Indeed, the highest conceit of man is to demand "how" and "why" Scripture is true before accepting it (Rom. 9:19-20). It reveals a commitment to the humanistic principle: *Man is the measure of all things - including God.*

One example of this is Clark Pinnock. In the book, *Predestination and FreeWill*, Pinnock uses the typical humanistic buzzwords such as "the demands of reason," etc., to indicate that *human reason unaided by Divine Revelation is the Origin of truth and meaning.* He condemns those who ignore the "demands of reason" by appealing to the incomprehensibility of God (p. 143). Instead, he offers a "rational hypothesis to explain sovereignty and freedom" that will satisfy "the requirements of intelligence" (p.144). His "rational hypothesis" will "require us to rethink aspects of conventional of classical theism" (p. 144). How do we know that his "rational hypothesis" is true? He refers to man's "intuition" and "reason" that can "sense" that it is true (p.150). Thus, he is perfectly "rational" to say, "I stand against classical theism" (p. 151).[2]

---

[1] For a detailed exegetical demonstration of the incomprehensibility of God, see my book: *The Trinity: Evidence and Issues* (World Pub. 1996), ppg 73-84.

[2] *Predestination and FreeWill*, eds. David Basinger and Randall Basinger (Downers Grove IL; InterVarsity Press, 1986). I document Pinnock's appeal to "reason" instead of Scripture in greater detail in my book, *Battle of the Gods.*

This is how you can always spot a humanist. He uses such phrases as:

It seems to me that…

I think that…

It is only rational that…

Intelligent people understand that…

Before the bar of reason…

My intuition tells me…

Common sense tells me that…

It is only reasonable that…

I do not see how…

It is not comprehensible to me that…, etc.

Biblical theologians do not accept the humanistic principle of human autonomy. They are committed to the opposite proposition: *God is the measure of all things - including man.* Without Divine Revelation, we can never know God.

> To the Law and to the Testimony! If they do not speak according to this Word, they have no light (Isa. 8:20).

With these brief words of introduction, we will now examine the Scriptures to see the self-disclosure of God concerning what He knows.

Part II

The Nature of God's Knowledge

If the authors of Scripture, under Divine inspiration, believed that God's knowledge could not be limited by anything, but was absolute Omniscience, how would they communicate that idea to their readers? This question must be answered before we even pick up the Bible. If we do not answer it, then we do not know what to look for and what to expect to find in Scripture. The following list reveals what we need to look for when we open the Bible.

- The Vocabulary of God's Knowledge
- The Fact of God's Knowledge
- The Nature of God's Knowledge
- The Primary Texts
- The Secondary Texts

The Vocabulary of God's Knowledge

If the authors of Scripture believed that God has knowledge of Himself and the world He created, we would expect to find them using those Hebrew and Greek words which would indicate to their readers that God has an intellect that is capable of understanding, comprehension and knowledge. In other words, we would expect to find that the God revealed in Scripture is a God of knowledge, not a god of ignorance.

Old Testament Vocabulary

In the Hebrew language there are several words that are used to speak of knowledge, understanding and comprehension.

A. The word יָדַע is the most common word for understanding and knowledge in the Hebrew Scriptures. It is used of man's knowledge and understanding hundreds of times. It is also applied to God to indicate that He has true knowledge of Himself and the world He created for His glory. (See: Exo. 3:7, 19-20; 2 Sam. 7:20; 1 Kings 8:39; Job 23:10; Psa. 31:7, 40:9, 69:5, Jer. 1:5, etc.)

B. The word בִּין is used to describe God's knowledge in Job 11:11, 28:23; Psa. 5:1, 33:15, 139:2. The wicked deny that God "takes notice" of their sin in Psa. 94:7b.

Neither shall the God of Jacob *notice it.*

לֹא־יָבִין אֱלֹהֵי יַעֲקֹב׃

C. The word דֵּעָה is used in 1 Sam. 2:3 in the phrase, "Yahweh is a God of knowledge" (אֵל דֵּעוֹת יְהוָה). The wicked used this word when questioning whether God knows anything.

"How doth God know?" (Psa. 73:11a).

אֵיכָה יָדַע־אֵל׃

D. The word חָזָה is used in Psa. 11:4,7 and Psa. 17:2 to indicate that God "sees" all things.

E. Another word for "consider," "behold," and "see" is רָאָה. It is applied to God's knowledge in Gen. 29:32,

31:42; Exo. 3:7, 4:31; Psa. 9:14, 10:11, 25:18,19, 84:10, 119:153,159. The wicked deny in Psa. 94:7 that God really sees anything.

> Yet they say, The LORD *shall not see.*
>
> וַיֹּאמְרוּ לֹא יִרְאֶה־יָּהּ

F. In Job 34:25, we told that God "takes knowledge of" (יַכִּיר) the works of man.

G. The Psalmist declared in Psa. 147:5, "His understanding is infinite."

> רַב־כֹּחַ לִתְבוּנָתוֹ אֵין מִסְפָּר׃

H. The biblical authors referred to "the eyes" of God to indicate that He sees all things. Nothing escapes His omniscient sight.

> For the eyes of the LORD run to and fro throughout the whole earth (2 Chron. 16:9).
>
> For my eyes are upon all their ways; they are not hid from my face, neither is their iniquity concealed from my eyes (Jer. 16:17).
>
> The eyes of the LORD, which run to and fro throughout the whole earth (Zech. 4:10).

The authors of the Hebrew Scriptures used every word in their vocabulary to affirm that God has knowledge. The only ones who deny or question this are the wicked.

New Testament Vocabulary

When we turn to the New Testament, the same pattern is followed. The common Greek words for knowledge, understanding and comprehension are applied to God without hesitation.

A. The common Greek verb for "knowing" is γινώσκω. It is applied to God in Lk. 16:15; John 10:15; 1 Cor. 3:20; Gal. 4:9; 2 Thess. 2:19; 1 Thess. 3:20 and 1 John 3:20.

B. The noun γνῶσις is used for God's knowledge in Rom. 11:33 where we are told that God's γνῶσις is incomprehensible.

C. In Acts 15:18, God's knowledge (γνωστα) is described as eternal (ἀπ' αἰῶνος).

D. Two different Greek words are used in the New Testament to signify God's foreknowledge of the future. The noun πρόγνωσίς (foreknowledge) is used in Acts 2:23 and 1 Pet. 1:2. The verb προγινώσκω (to foreknow) is used in Rom. 8:29; 11:2 and 1 Pet. 1:20.

E. In Greek, the word for intellect or mind is νοῦς. It is used of God in Rom. 11:34 and 1 Cor. 2:16.

F. The Greek verb οἶδα means "to know" and is used of God in 2 Cor. 11:11; 12:3 and 2 Pet. 2:9.

G. The noetic sense of "seeing" is expressed by the Greek word βλέπω and is used in Mat. 6:6 to refer to God's seeing us wherever we are.

H. The authors of the New Testament, like the authors of the Old Testament, used every word that existed in the language of their day to convey the idea that God knows Himself and the world He made.

The Fact of God's Knowledge

The nouns and verbs used for God's knowledge in both the Old and New Testaments is sufficient to establish its factuality beyond all doubt. This doctrine played a significant role in the life of the believer. In her prayer, Hannah states in a matter of fact manner,

> "The LORD is a God of knowledge" (1 Sam. 2:3).
>
> אֵל דֵּעוֹת יְהוָה
>
> θεὸς <u>γνώσεων</u> κύριος

Notice that in both the Hebrew (דֵּעוֹת) and the Greek (γνώσεων) text, the word "knowledge" is actually in the plural. This indicates that Yahweh is the God of "*knowledges*;" i.e., all knowledge. She argues in her prayer that because He is "a God of knowledges," there is no God like Him (v. 2.). To her the very idea that God was ignorant would have been blasphemous. How could He judge the world if He were ignorant? (vs. 3-10).

Throughout the Psalms, God is addressed as the One who knows all things. In Psa. 139 David said in verse 2,

> "You know when I sit down and when I rise up; You understand my thoughts from afar."

In verse 6, David concludes,

> "Such knowledge is too wonderful for me; It is too high, I cannot attain to it."

Several comments are in order. First, the fact of God's knowledge is assumed to be true. Second, the extent of it is revealed. Third, David concludes that God's knowledge is a subject beyond the capacity of his finite mind to understand. It is "too high" and "too wonderful." Even though David could not explain "how" or "why" God knows all things, this did not make the doctrine odious to him. Instead, it caused David to fall at God's feet in worship, awe and praise.

The New Testament is just as committed to the fact of God being a God of knowledge. When Paul encountered a situation which exceeded his capacity to understand, he would rest in the fact that ὁ θεὸς οἶδεν "*God knows*" (2 Cor. 12:3). Paul makes it clear that God knows the truth even when we do not. See also 2 Cor. 11:11 where Paul appeals to the fact that ὁ θεὸς οἶδεν "God knows."

The Nature of God's Knowledge

The nature of God's knowledge is directly addressed in both Testaments. Instead of sitting in a dark room trying to figure out what He can or cannot know by our own limited intelligence, why not turn to the light of Scripture?

Perfect in Knowledge

First, God's knowledge is תְּמִים "*perfect*" according to Job 37:16.

> "The wondrous works of *Him who is perfect in knowledge.*"

הֲתֵדַע עַל־מִפְלְשֵׂי־עָב מִפְלְאוֹת תְּמִים דֵּעִים׃

The perfection of God's knowledge means that it is not deficient in anything for "he who is perfect is not lacking in anything."

> τέλειοι καὶ ὁλόκληροι ἐν μηδενὶ λειπόμενοι (James 1:4).

God's knowledge is thus *complete* and *nothing need be added to it.* This means that God's knowledge is *self-existent* and *independent* of anything outside of His own divine nature. He does not need to use logic or the scientific method to discover Truth. His knowledge is one, unified, single, perfect vision of all things from the end to the beginning of the creation from all eternity. Paul tells us that God is not in need of anything because He is perfect in every respect (Acts 17:25).

He Does Not Need Your Information

Because God's knowledge is perfect, He is not in need of any information from us.

> "Can any one teach God knowledge, Seeing
> He judgeth those that are high?" (Job 21:22).
>
> הַלְאֵל יְלַמֶּד־דָּעַת וְהוּא רָמִים יִשְׁפּוֹט׃
>
> πότερον οὐχὶ ὁ κύριός ἐστιν ὁ διδάσκων
>
> σύνεσιν καὶ ἐπιστήμην αὐτὸς δὲ φόνους
>
> διακρινεῖ

In order for God to judge man on the Day of Judgment, He has to have perfect knowledge of all things. This is why God is not in need of someone to give Him counsel, which is information and advice (Rom. 11:34).

> "Who has known the mind of the Lord?"
>
> Τίς γὰρ ἔγνω νοῦν κυρίου;
>
> "Who has become his adviser?"
>
> ἢ τίς σύμβουλος αὐτοῦ ἐγένετο;

It Does Not Increase or Decrease

Since His knowledge is perfect, it cannot increase or decrease. It is complete and whole. He does not have to investigate to find out anything.

> "He sees iniquity *without investigation.*"
>
> וַיַּרְא־אָוֶן וְלֹא יִתְבּוֹנָן׃ (Job 11:11)
>
> "For *He does not have to wait for the results*

of a judicial investigation to regard a man."
(Translation K&D, Job II:255-256)

כִּי לֹא עַל־אִישׁ יָשִׂים עוֹד לַהֲלֹךְ
אֶל־אֵל בַּמִּשְׁפָּט׃ (Job. 34:23)

"He will break mighty men w*ithout inquiry*
and puts others in their place."

יָרֹעַ כַּבִּירִים לֹא־חֵקֶר וַיַּעֲמֵד אֲחֵרִים
תַּחְתָּם׃ (Job 34:24)

But don't we have to tell God in prayer what we need? If we don't tell Him, how will He know what we want? The purpose of prayer is not to inform God of your needs. He knows what you need and what you are going to say before you say it. Prayer is for our benefit, not God's information.

"Your *Father knows* what you need *before you ask him*" (Mat. 6:8).

οἶδεν γὰρ ὁ πατὴρ ὑμῶν ὧν χρείαν ἔχετε
πρὸ τοῦ ὑμᾶς αἰτῆσαι αὐτόν.

"Even *before there is a word on my tongue*, behold, O LORD, *you know everything*" (Psa. 139:4).

כִּי אֵין מִלָּה בִּלְשׁוֹנִי הֵן יְהוָה יָדַעְתָּ כֻלָּהּ׃

It Is Infinite

Since His knowledge is perfect, it is no surprise to us to find that it is *infinite* according to Psa. 147:5.

> His understanding is *infinite.*
>
> לִתְבוּנָתוֹ אֵין. מִסְפָּר

Being "infinite" means that we cannot place any limitations on His knowledge. There is no "cutting off" place where we can say that His knowledge begins or ends.

It Is Eternal

Since it is infinite, God's knowledge is *eternal.* In Acts 15:18, James reminded the counsel that the inclusion of the Gentiles into the church did not catch God by surprise. God had known (γνωστα) everything from eternity (ἀπ' αἰῶνος). God does not have to wait until the end to see what will happen like we do. He knows "the end from the beginning" (Isa. 46:10).

It Is Immutable

Being perfect, infinite and eternal, God's knowledge is *immutable* (Mal. 3:6; James 1:17). Because it is immutable, God cannot make a mistake; He cannot lie; He does not change His mind.

> God is not a man, that *he should lie*; neither the son of man, that *he should change His mind*: *hath he said, and shall he not do it? Or hath he spoken, and shall he not make it good*? (Num. 23:19).
>
> And also the Strength of Israel *will not lie nor repent:* for he *is* not a man, that *he should change His mind* (1 Sam. 15:29).

> The hope of eternal life that God, *who cannot lie*, promised before the world began (Tit. 1:2).

> In the same way, when God wanted to make the *unchangeble character of his purpose* perfectly clear to the heirs of his promise, he guaranteed it with an oath so that by these two *unchangeble* things, in which it is *impossible for God to prove false*, we who have taken refuge in him might have a strong encouragement to take hold of the hope set befrore us (Heb. 6:17-18).

Several comments should be made on the passages above. First, the authors of Scripture repeatedly emphasize that God is not a man and thus His knowledge is not limited or flawed as man's knowledge. This is stressed in other passages as well.

> But the LORD said unto Samuel, Look not on his countenance, or on the height of his stature; because I have refused him: for *the LORD seeth not as man seeth; for man looketh on the outward appearance, but the LORD looketh on the heart* (1 Sam. 16:7).

> *Do You have eyes of flesh? or do You see as man sees? Are Your days as the days of man? Are Your years as man's days, that You have to inquire after my iniquity, and search after my sin?* (Job 10:4-7).

> For My thoughts are not your thoughts, neither are your ways My ways, saith the LORD. For as the heavens are higher than the earth, so are My ways higher than your ways,

> and My thoughts than your thoughts (Isa. 55:8-9).

The main reason why humanists are always trying to limit the knowledge of God is to bring God down to the level of man. They have forgotten God's stern rebuke,

> You thought that I was altogether such a one as yourself: But I will reprove you, and set them in order before your eyes (Psa. 50:21).

Since God's knowledge is absolute and unlimited, He is incapable of lying. Notice that Heb. 6:17-18 clearly links together God's immutability and omniscience in such a way that you cannot have one without the other. Thus God's knowledge is *infallible* and cannot err in any sense.

It Is Clear , Distinct, Certain And Orderly

Since God's knowledge is perfect in all aspects, it is *clear* instead of unclear, *distinct* instead of vague, *certain* instead of uncertain, and *orderly* instead of chaotic for God is not a God of confusion, but of harmony.

> οὐ γάρ ἐστιν ἀκαταστασίας ὁ θεὸς ἀλλὰ εἰρήνης. (1 Cor. 14:33).

It Is Infallible

Is God's knowledge an "iffy" thing that may or may not pan out as the future unfolds? Does the *infallibility* of God's knowledge mean that the future must *necessarily* happen as He knows it? In order for the future *necessarily* to happen as God sees it, must it be *certain, fixed, preordained and predetermined* from eternity? Is anything left to luck or chance?

How can we answer such deep questions? *Sola Scriptura*! Scripture alone can give us God's answers to such questions. Why? First, human reason is not adequate to come up with an answer because the world with all its philosophic reasoning and logic never knew the true God (1 Cor. 1:21). Second, Paul warns us that speculative theology, in which you try to figure out God by your own intellect instead of going to Scripture, produces nothing but pride and conceit.

> Now these things, brethren, I have in a figure transferred to myself and Apollos for your sakes; that in us ye might learn, "*Do not go beyond what is Written*," that no one of you should be puffed up for the one against the other (1 Cor. 4:6).
>
> Ταῦτα δέ, ἀδελφοί, μετεσχημάτισα εἰς ἐμαυτὸν καὶ Ἀπολλῶν δι' ὑμᾶς, ἵνα ἐν ἡμῖν μάθητε τὸ Μὴ ὑπὲρ ἃ γέγραπται, ἵνα μὴ εἷς ὑπὲρ τοῦ ἑνὸς φυσιοῦσθε κατὰ τοῦ ἑτέρου.

If the authors of Scripture believed that the future, including the decisions and works of man, is already *fixed, certain, preordained* and *predetermined*, and, at the same time, that man is *accountable* to God for his thoughts, words and deeds, how would they convey that idea to their readers? By what vocabulary? By what exegesis?

What if we find that they held to the *certainty* and *necessity* of the future and that man was *accountable* at the same time? Just because pagan Greek philosophy taught that man is not accountable if his actions are predetermined, are we to throw the Bible in the trash and follow the philosophers instead of Scripture?

To answer the questions stated above, all we have to find is just *one* passage in the Bible where the acts of a man were both predetermined and accountable at the same time. Why? If Divine predetermination and human accountability are both revealed in Scripture, then in principle both truths are *compatible*; i.e., *not contradictory*.

This is why the historic Christian view is sometimes called the "compatibility" view and the contrary views are called the "contradictory" views. If the authors of Scripture believed and taught that Divine predetermination and human accountability were compatible truths because God understood how they were compatible even though man does not, on what grounds can those who claim to be Christians state that the two doctrines are incompatible and thus inherently contradictory to God as well as man? On what grounds do they limit God's ability to understand what He has revealed in Scripture?

First, did the authors of Scripture ever describe the future, including the acts of man as "certain," "necessary," "determined," "fixed," "foreordained" or "appointed"? Did they ever say that future "must" happened? Is the future "certain"? Or is it up to the roll of the dice in some kind of cosmic crap game?

The Exodus Prediction

> And He said unto Abram, *Know for certain* that your seed *shall* be sojourners in a land that is not theirs, and they *shall* serve them; and they *shall* afflict them four hundred years; And also that nation, whom they shall serve, I *will judge*: and afterward they *shall* come out with great substance (Gen. 15:13-14).

The passage above is remarkable in that it catches up all the decisions and acts of all the people involved in the move to Egypt, the enslavement and oppression of the Jews, the coming of Moses and the events leading to the Exodus. God told Abraham that all these things were "certain" to happen. The use of "shall" and "will" instead of "may" or "might" reveals that all these future things would happen just as God said they would.

If these future events were *certain* to happen, then Abraham's knowledge of them would likewise be *certain.* You cannot have certain knowledge of that which is fundamentally uncertain. Thus God told Abraham that he could count on this prediction of future events coming true.

The Story of Joseph

That this is what Moses understood is clear from his account of Joseph in Genesis chapters 38-50. The decision of his brothers to beat him and then sell him into slavery, the slave masters taking him to Egypt instead of some other country, the false rape charge made by Potiphar's wife, his prison experience, his rise to Pharoah's side and the decision of Jacob to move to Egpyt; were all these decisions and acts of all the people involved autonomous; i.e., were they independent of God? Can we really describe them in terms of mere coincidence and luck? Was Joseph just unlucky when he experienced bad things and lucky when he experienced good things? Was it merely by chance that the jailer liked him? Was it really a mere coincidence that Pharaoh made him second to himself?

Instead of sitting around speculating, let us turn to the testimony of Joseph to see what he believed.

> But as for you, you thought to do evil against me; *but God meant it unto good*, to bring to pass, as *it is* this day, to save many people alive (Gen. 50:20).

Can words be clearer? Did not Joseph believe that God planned *everything* including what his brothers did to him in order to save many people from starvation? Did he believe that *everything* that happened to him happened *necessarily as part of God's plan*? Why did Potiphar like Joseph? Moses tells us,

> And his master saw that the LORD was with him, and that the LORD *caused* all that he did to prosper in his hand (Gen. 39:3).
>
> וַיַּרְא אֲדֹנָיו כִּי יְהוָה אִתּוֹ וְכֹל אֲשֶׁר־הוּא עֹשֶׂה יְהוָה מַצְלִיחַ בְּיָדוֹ׃
>
> ᾔδει δὲ ὁ κύριος αὐτοῦ ὅτι κύριος μετ' αὐτοῦ καὶ ὅσα ἂν ποιῇ κύριος εὐοδοῖ ἐν ταῖς χερσὶν αὐτοῦ

According to Moses, "Yahweh caused" (Heb. מַצְלִיחַ יְהוָה Gk. ποιῇ κύριος) everything Joseph did to prosper. Joseph believed that God was in control of the entire situation.

But did the belief that God planned the whole thing in any way lessen, negate or reduce the responsibility of all those involved? No. The brothers admitted that their decisions and actions that led to selling Joseph into slavery were wicked and evil. They knew that they were responsible for what they did. They knew that they deserved punishment.

> So shall you say unto Joseph, Forgive, I pray you now, *the transgression of your brothers, and their sin, for what they did unto you was evil.* And now, we beg you, forgive the transgression of the servants of the God of your father. And Joseph wept as they spoke unto him (Gen. 50:17).

Joseph agreed that they had intended to do evil to him. BUT everything they did was also part of a bigger picture. Namely, the sovereign purpose and plan of God. As Joseph looked back at his life with all its ups and downs, he saw the hand of God behind it all.

David and the Philistines

> And David inquired of the LORD, saying, "Shall I go up against the Philistines? *Will You deliver them into my hand*?" And the LORD said unto David, "Go up; for *I will certainly deliver* the Philistines into thy hand" (2 Sam. 5:19).

What was going to happen when David entered into battle with the Philistines? Was there the possibility that the Philistines would win and David lose? Was it only up to the decisions of all the men involved and to Lady Luck as to who would decide to run away in defeat? Could things turn out in any different way? Or was the future battle "certain" to happen just as God said, because God would see to it? Did God interfere in the affairs of men to determine who would win the battle? Was the final outcome of the battle already "certain" before David left camp? The passage is quite clear that David's victory was already certain and "in the bag" before he picked up his spear.

Death Awaits You

> The LORD had showed me that he *shall certainly die* (2 Kings 8:10).

Hazel wanted to know if he would in the future recover from his illness. He asked the prophet of the LORD and was told that he "shall certainly die." But was this already set in stone? Could not something happen that would heal Hazel? Or was his death already *certain*? It was as certain as God lives.

The Babylonian Capivity

> The king of Babylon shall *certainly* come and destroy this land, and shall cause to cease from thence man and beast (Jer. 36:29).

> Thus says the LORD, "This city shall *certainly* be given into the hand of the army of the king of Babylon, and he shall take it (Jer. 38:3).
>
> But seek not Beth-el, nor enter into Gilgal, and pass not to Beer-sheba: for Gilgal shall *certainly* go into captivity, and Beth-el *shall come* to nought (Amos 5:5).
>
> For thus Amos said, "Jeroboam *shall die* by the sword, and Israel shall *certainly* be led away captive out of their own land (Amos 7:11).
>
> Israel shall *certainly* go into captivity (Amos 7:17).

Was the invasion of Babylon and the captivity *certain* to happen in the future? Couldn't the king suddenly decide not to invade Israel? Wasn't there the possibility that Israel would defeat the Babylonians? No. It was already *certain* before the Babylonians climbed into their chariots.

Would Jeremiah Die?

> For I will *certainly* deliver you, and you *shall not* fall by the sword (Jer. 39:18).

How could God guarantee Jeremiah that the future would turn out as He said it would? Was it really "certain" and already "fixed" that Jeremiah would not die? Could some Babylonian soldier suddenly decide to run his sword through Jeremiah? No. God would interfere and see to it that Jeremiah would not be harmed.

Future Events Already Appointed

> For the vision is yet for the *appointed time*, and it hasteth toward the end, and *shall not lie*:

> though it tarry, wait for it; because it will *certainly* come, it will not delay (Hab. 2:3).

Since the captivity has been "appointed" by God, it will *certainly* come to pass in the future in exactly the way God said it would happen. If future events could turn out differently than the vision stated, then God would be guilty of telling *a lie*.

Are future events fixed?

> He answered them, "It is not for you to know what times or seasons *the Father has fixed* by His own authority (Acts 1:7).

> εἶπεν δὲ πρὸς αὐτούς, Οὐχ ὑμῶν ἐστιν γνῶναι χρόνους ἢ καιροὺς οὓς ὁ πατὴρ ἔθετο ἐν τῇ ἰδίᾳ ἐξουσίᾳ,

Jesus pointed out to the disciples that the future has already been "fixed" by the Father. The word ἔθετο is a second aorist middle indicative and emphasizes the sovereignty of the Father over time.

> For he *has fixed a day* when he is going to judge the world with justice through a man he has appointed (Acts 17:31).

> καθότι ἔστησεν ἡμέραν ἐν ᾗ μέλλει κρίνειν τὴν οἰκουμένην ἐν δικαιοσύνῃ ἐν ἀνδρὶ ᾧ ὥρισεν, πίστιν παρασχὼν πᾶσιν ἀναστήσας αὐτὸν ἐκ νεκρῶν.

The Day of Judgment has already been fixed by the Father. It is an appointment that we all have to meet. But is there not the possibility that something could happen that God did not foresee and that would cancel or change the Day of Judgment? No. It is "set in stone" and cannot tarry or be overthrown.

> From one man he made every nation of humanity to live all over the earth, *fixing the seasons of the year and the boundaries they live in* (Acts 17:26).
>
> ἐποίησέν τε ἐξ ἑνὸς πᾶν ἔθνος ἀνθρώπων κατοικεῖν ἐπὶ παντὸς προσώπου τῆς γῆς, ὁρίσας προστεταγμένους καιροὺς καὶ τὰς ὁροθεσίας τῆς κατοικίας αὐτῶν

If man were free in the Greek ideal of absolute human autonomy, then he would be absolutely free to choose when and where he lives. But Paul says that the time and place of your birth and your habitation is something that God determines and appoints before you were ever born.

Are Future Events Going to Happen Necessarily?

Did anyone ever do anything that was "necessary" for him to do it according to the preordained plan and purpose of God? This question is so important that only special revelation can answer it.

> *Was it not necessary* for the Christ to suffer these things, and to enter into his glory? (Luke 24:26).
>
> οὐχὶ ταῦτα ἔδει παθεῖν τὸν Χριστὸν καὶ εἰσελθεῖν εἰς τὴν δόξαν αὐτοῦ;

Was it *necessary* for Judas to betray Christ? For the Romans to deliver Him to death? For the Jewish leaders to demand His death? For the soldier to pierce His side with a spear? Did all the choices of everyone involved take place *necessarily*? Was it all mere coincidence? Was there a chance that He would not have been arrested, tried, tortured and crucified or did those things have to done by all those involved because it was *necessary*? If they did things because they had to; i.e., it was *necessary*, were they held accountable to God for what they did? The present text and the next one answer these questions.

> Brothers, *it was necessary for the Scripture to be fulfilled*, which the Holy Spirit spoke long ago through the mouth of David about *Judas*, who was the guide to those who arrested Jesus (Acts 1:16).
>
> Ανδρες ἀδελφοί, ἔδει πληρωθῆναι τὴν γραφὴν ἣν προεῖπεν τὸ πνεῦμα τὸ ἅγιον διὰ στόματος Δαυὶδ περὶ Ἰούδα τοῦ γενομένου ὁδηγοῦ τοῖς συλλαβοῦσιν Ἰησοῦν,

Luke tells us that all the choices and decisions of man that came together to cause the death of Christ, including the decision of Judas to betray the Lord, were done *necessarily.*

> Explaining and showing that *it was necessary* that the Christ *should suffer*, and *to rise again from the dead* (Acts 17:3).
>
> διανοίγων καὶ παρατιθέμενος ὅτι τὸν Χριστὸν ἔδει παθεῖν καὶ ἀναστῆναι ἐκ νεκρῶν καὶ ὅτι οὗ τός ἐστιν ὁ Χριστός [ὁ] Ἰησοῦς ὃν ἐγὼ καταγγέλλω ὑμῖν.

Was Christ's death at the hands of sinners a matter of bad luck, a chance happening, a mere coincidence? No. All those things happened because it was *necessary* for these things to take place. They were part of God's eternal plan of the ages.

Are Future Events Ever Predetermined?

Do the biblical authors say that someone ever chose to do something that was *predetermined* that he should chose to do it?

> For the Son of man is going away, *as it has been predetermined*: *but how terrible it will be for that man by whom He is betrayed!* (Lk. 22:22).
>
> ὅτι ὁ υἱὸς μὲν τοῦ ἀνθρώπου κατὰ τὸ ὡρισμένον πορεύεται, πλὴν οὐαὶ τῷ ἀνθρώπῳ ἐκείνῳ δι' οὗ παραδίδοται.

When Judas chose to betray the Lord, was his choice *predetermined*? If Luke was inspired by God to write his Gospel account, then we have to accept the fact that he clearly stated that Judas' betrayal was something that had been predetermined. But, we hasten to add, lest anyone foolishly think that this meant that Judas was not responsible for his actions, Luke adds, "Woe unto that man through whom He is betrayed." There is no indication in the text to suggest that Luke had a problem believing that the choices and actions of Judas were determined and that he was responsible at the same time. These two were compatible and not contradictory.

> Him, being delivered up by the *predetermined* counsel and foreknowledge of God, you by the hand of lawless men did crucify and slay (Acts 2:23).
>
> τοῦτον τῇ ὡρισμένῃ βουλῇ καὶ προγνώσει τοῦ θεοῦ ἔκδοτον διὰ χειρὸς ἀνόμων προσπήξαντες ἀνείλατε

The men who crucified the Lord did not know that what they did was predetermined by God before time began. *They are responsible for what was predetermined for them to do.* Peter did not give any indication that he was bothered with these revealed truths. They were compatible in his eyes.

What About Predestination?

If the biblical authors believed that the future was predetermined, we would expect them to use such words as "predestination." Did they ever use such terminology when describing the future acts of men?

> For of a truth in this city against thy holy Servant Jesus, whom You did anoint, both Herod and Pontius Pilate, with the Gentiles and the peoples of Israel, were gathered together, *to do whatsoever thy hand and thy council predestined to come to pass* (Acts 4:27-28).
>
> ποιῆσαι ὅσα ἡ χείρ σου καὶ ἡ βουλή [σου] <u>προώρισεν γενέσθαι.</u>

Do you really believe that every word in the Bible is God's Word? Then, regardless of how you feel about it, you have to accept the fact that such words as "predestination," "election," and "predetermined" are found in the Bible. Those who had a hand in putting to death the Son of God are held accountable for what they did and, at the same time, what they did was predestined by God from eternity that they should do it. The text cannot be dismissed by saying that God *knew* that they would do it. The word προώρισεν means to predestine or predetermine that certain things will be done in the future.

Must the Future Happen?

Does the Bible ever say that the future acts of a man "must" happen?

> From that time began Jesus to show unto His disciples, that He *must go* to Jerusalem, and *suffer many things* of the elders and chief priests and scribes, and *be killed*, and the third day *be raised up* (Matt. 16:21).

Jesus "must" go, suffer, die and be raised. Why? It was the Father's plan for Him to die on the cross. The same statement is repeated in Mark 8:31.

What about "end times" predictions? Will the future events happen because they *must* happen?

> And you are going to hear of wars and rumors of wars. See to it that you are not alarmed. *These things must take place;* but that's not the end (Matt. 24:6).

The decisions and actions of men that are predicted in Matt. 24 "must" happen as God says they will happen.

Is the Future Open to Change?

If the future were open to change, then the Bible could *not* describe future events as happening necessarily. But if it does speak of future events as necessarily happening, then this is clear indication that the writers believed that the future was fixed.

> Acts 23:11, "Y*ou must testify* in Rome."

> Acts 27:24, "You *must* stand before the emperor."

Paul was told that God had decided that he was going to witness to Caesar in Rome. The future had already been fixed and predetermined. Not even a shipwreck could prevent the trip to Rome. Paul was immortal until he had completed his destiny. These are but a few of the passages in the Bible that speak of future events, including the acts of man, as things that "must" happen.

Are Future Events "Destined" By God?

> When the Gentiles heard this, they began rejoicing and glorifying the word of the Lord. Meanwhile, *all who had been destined to eternal life believed* (Acts 13:48).
>
> ἀκούοντα δὲ τὰ ἔθνη ἔχαιρον καὶ ἐδόξαζον τὸν λόγον τοῦ κυρίου καὶ ἐπίστευσαν ὅσοι ἦσαν τεταγμένοι εἰς ζωὴν αἰώνιον·

Luke clearly states that those who had been "destined to eternal life" believed. Their decision to believe is something that God "destined" them to do.

> They keep on stumbling because they disobey the Word, as *they were destined to do* (1 Pet. 2:8).
>
> καὶ λίθος προσκόμματος καὶ πέτρα σκανδάλου· οἳ προσκόπτουσιν τῷ λόγῳ ἀπειθοῦντες εἰς ὃ καὶ ἐτέθησαν.

We have to deal with what Peter says in this verse without violating the grammar and syntax of the Greek text. He says that those who decided to disobey the Lord were "destined" to do this. Jude says the same thing (Jude 4). The words must mean something.

Are Future Events "Ordained" and "Preordained"?

Do the authors of the Bible ever trace man's decisions and actions back to God's preordination?

> And Absalom and all the men of Israel said, "The counsel of Hushai the Archite is better than the counsel of Ahithophel. *For the LORD had ordained to defeat the good counsel of Ahithophel,*

> *to the intent that the LORD might bring disaster upon Absalom* (2 Sam. 17:14).

This passage is remarkable. It answers the questions, "Why did Absalom and all the men of Israel *choose* not to listen to Athithophel when he was clearly the wisest counselor in their midst? Why did they *choose* to take Hushai's advice instead? The text states that God caused them to choose Hushai because *He had ordained* to defeat Absolom. *They chose what He ordained them to choose.*

It Is Incomprehensible to Man

Since God's knowledge is perfect, infinite, eternal and immutable, it is no surprise that it is also *incomprehensible.* How God can know the end of eternity at the beginning of eternity is beyond our capacity to understand or to explain. But this what the Bible teaches.

> Have you not known? Have you not heard, that the everlasting God, the LORD, the Creator of the ends of the earth, fainteth not, neither is weary? That *His understanding is incomprehensible?* (Isa. 40:28).

> O how deep are God's riches, wisdom and knowledge! *How impossible to explain his judgments or to understand his ways*! (Rom. 11:33).

When the humanists in Augustine's day objected to the Gospel by saying, "I will not believe until I understand," Augustine replied, "I believe in order that I may understand."

Secondary Texts

The Wicked and God's Knowledge

Today, many theologians and philosophers question and even deny the fact of God's omniscience. They boast that they are on the "cutting edge" of modern theology. But they are merely following in the footsteps of people whom the Bible describes as "the wicked."

> Is not God in the height of heaven? Look also at the distant stars, how high they are. And you say, "*What does God know? How He can judge through thick darkness? Clouds are a hiding place for Him, so that He cannot see;* and He walks on the vault of heaven" (Job 22:12-13).

Eliphaz rebukes the arrogance of thinking that God is so transcendent that He cannot know what is happening on earth. He ridicules the idea that darkness and clouds can prevent God from seeing what is happening on earth.

> And they say, "*How does God know? And is there knowledge with the Most High?*" Behold, these are the wicked (Psa. 73:11-12).

Notice that the challenge is given to explain "how" God knows. Since no one can fully explain how God knows *anything*, much less *everything*, the wicked go on to question whether God has any knowledge at all.

> And they say, "*The LORD does not see. Nor does the God of Jacob pay heed*" (Psa. 94:7).

The denial of God's knowledge is used as a reason for not being afraid of the judgment of God. He will not take notice of our sin, so don't worry about it.

> Why do you say, O Jacob, and assert, O Israel, "*My way is hidden from the LORD*. And the justice due me escapes the notice of my God?" (Isa. 40:27).

Some people in Isaiah's day cast doubt on the knowledge of God by claiming that their sins were "hidden" from God and thus He did not "take notice" of them.

Who are these people who question the fact of God's knowledge? The prophets? No. The righteous? No. Those who love the Lord? No. In each context where the knowledge of God is questioned, it is always the *wicked* who cast doubt on God's knowledge. They are the ones who demand that the righteous tell them "how" and "why" God knows. When the righteous fail to do so, this is used as the basis to reject revealed truth.

The wicked today are just as bold in casting doubt on God's knowledge. They have searched the Bible for texts which indicate to them that God is ignorant. They use the following secondary texts to contradict the clear teaching of the primary texts.

Does God Know Where You Are?

> Then the LORD God called to the man, and said to him, "Where are you?" And He said, "Who told you that you were naked? Have you eaten from the tree of which I commanded you not to eat?" (Gen. 3:9,11).

These passages indicate to humanistic theologians that God was ignorant not only of the whereabouts of Adam and Eve but also of their sin. They assume that the questions God asked revealed His ignorance. But is this really what is taught in this passage? Are not the questions asked for man's sake so that he might confess his sin? If this secondary text could overthrow the knowledge of God, it would mean that God has no present knowledge of where we are and no past knowledge of what we have done. Prayer would be useless and the Judgment Day impossible. Some philosophers have attempted to use this passage to prove that God cannot know the future. Why they do this is beyond us. The passage is clearly speaking of the *present* whereabouts of Adam and his *past* transgression. God did not ask, "Where will you be tomorrow?" If this Scripture were taken literally, God would not know the past or the present!

Does God See You?

> And the LORD came down to see the city and the tower, which the sons of men had built (Gen. 11:5).

It is claimed that this passage teaches that God was ignorant of what man was doing. Thus, He had to travel down to earth to see what was going on. If taken literally, it would not only deny the omniscience of God but also His *omnipresence.* In order to find out what was going on, God had to leave heaven and travel to earth in order to gain knowledge. He would not be everywhere present but would be a creature of time and space.

But this would overthrow all the primary texts which clearly teach that God is omnipresent as well as omniscient (Psa. 139:7-12). Prayer would be a stupid ritual because unless God happened to pass by at the time you were praying, He would not know that you were praying.

This is a passage that also is used by some philosophers to prove that God does not know the future. But once again, it is the knowledge of the *past* and *present* that is in view. God did not go down to see what they *were* going to do but what man *had* done and *was* doing at that time.

Sodom and Gomorrah

> And the LORD said, "The outcry of Sodom and Gomorrah is indeed great, and their sin is exceedingly grave. I will go down now, and see if they have done entirely according to the outcry, which has come to Me; and, if not, I will know (Gen. 18:20-21).

Once again, if taken literally, the omnipresence of God as well as His omniscience would be denied. God had to go and see if the rumor He had heard was true. And, if He discovered that it was not true, then He would know it. But does God really have to travel to the site of sin to know about it? Does He have to run here and there to investigate rumors? No. Such primary texts as Job 11:11 state that "He sees iniquity *without investigating*" (יַּרְא־אָוֶן וְלֹא יִתְבּוֹנָן׃).

Does God Know Our Hearts?

> "...now I know that you fear God" (Gen. 22:12).

If taken literally, not until Abraham passed the test did the angel of the LORD (a theophany of the Son of God) know the spiritual condition of Abraham's heart. Yet, there are dozens of primary passages which state that God does know the spiritual condition of the heart.

> You alone *know the hearts of all the sons of men* (1 Kings 8:39).

> God sees not as man sees, for man looks at the outward appearance, but the LORD *looks at the he*art (1 Sam. 16:7).

Some humanistic theologians and philosophers have used this passage to prove (sic) that Abraham changed the future. They assume that when God told Abraham to kill his son, that is what God had ordained to happen in the future, but Abraham's obedience changed God's mind and the future at the same time.

That this interpretation is absurd is obvious from the fact that while Abraham was going up one side of the mountain, a ram was climbing up the other side to be the substitute sacrifice (v.13). God provided the ram because:

(a.) He never decreed that Isaac would be killed;

(b.) He knew that Abraham would discover that the most precious person in his life was God, not his son;

(c.) A ram would be sacrificed instead of Isaac.

Failed Expectations?

> What more was there to do for My vineyard that I have not done in it? Why, when I expected it to produce good grapes did it produce worthless ones? (Isa. 5:4).

It is claimed that this passage teaches that God was ignorant that Israel was not going to bear good fruit. His expectations were not met because He did not know the future. If taken literally, it would portray a pathetic, impotent god! The poor thing is constantly frustrated by unforeseen events that fail to meet his expectations. But this would contradict dozens of primary passages that clearly establish the omniscience of God. In the same book, Isaiah says that God "declares the end from the beginning" (Isa. 46:10). Thus, whatever Isa. 5:4 means it cannot be twisted to contradict what the author elsewhere clearly teaches.

Is God Absent-Minded?

> Their sin I will remember no more (Jer. 31:34).

If taken literally, this text suggests to some philosophers that God can forget the past. But does God have lapses of memory like we do? Or is this verse to be interpreted in some other way? There are dozens of primary texts that indicate that God never "forgets" the past in the sense of a lapse of memory. The Day of Judgment would be impossible without God's omniscient knowledge of the past with all of its sins.

The word "remember" is used in its *judicial* sense that God will not legally hold our sins against us because the Messiah took the punishment for those sins in our place (Isa. 53:4-6).

It Never Entered God's Mind

> And they built the high places of Baal that are in the valley of Ben-hinnom to cause their sons and their daughters to pass through the fire to Molech, which I had not commanded them nor had it entered My Mind that they should do this abomination, to cause Judah to sin (Jer. 32:35).

Some philosophers have used this text to say that God was ignorant of the future human sacrifices that would take place in the valley of Ben-hinnom. It never entered His mind that such an abomination would take place. But is this really what the passage is saying? No. The passage is simply stating that God never told them to kill their children and that *it never crossed His mind to tell them to do so.* The Hebrew grammar is clear on this point.

To Know Is To Love

> You only have I known among the families of the earth (Amos 3:2).

If taken literally, some have urged that God admits that His knowledge is limited to the nation of Israel and that He is ignorant of other nations. Yet, is not the word for "known" (יָדַע) used for the *love relationship* between a man and his wife? (Gen. 4:1). Is not Israel described as the "wife" of Yahweh? Is not God here speaking of His special love relationship to Israel? Yes.

The Day of Judgment

> Then I'll tell you plainly, "I never knew you. Get away from me, you evidoers!" (Matt. 7:23).

If we take these words literally, then Christ on the day of judgment will admit that He was ignorant of the existence of many people. Yet, if Christ were here admitting that He was ignorant of them, on what basis did He send them to hell? He says to them, "Get away from me, you evidoers!" Evidently, He knows of their sin and will send them to hell for it. Doesn't the context indicate that Jesus was using the Hebrew meaning of the word "know"? Thus, He never had *a personal love relationship* with these people. We think so.

Does God Repent?

What about the passages where God is said in the King James Version to "repent"? (Gen. 6:6-7; Exo. 32:14; Jud. 2:18; 1 Sam. 15:11,35; 2 Sam. 24:16; 1 Chron. 21:15; Psa. 106:45; Jer. 26:19; Joel 2:13; Amos 7:3,6; Jonah 3:9-10; 4:2). Do these passages prove that the future is unknown to God?

Do they prove that God changes His "mind" (i.e., eternal decrees) about the future?

First, if we take the King James Version translation and give it a literal interpretation, it would appear that God "repented" of **sin**. This would not bother Stephen Davis, associate professor of philosophy at Claremont College. He has argued that God can sin, God can lie, and even break His promises![1] Luckily for us, He has not done these things so far.

But is this what these passages mean? Is there a GOD above God to whom He is accountable? To whom does God repent and whose forgiveness does He seek? The Bible clearly states in many places that "God *cannot* lie" (Num. 23:19: Tit. 1:2). He *cannot* even be tempted to sin, much less be guilty of sin (James 1:13). Thus whatever the KJV meant by the word "repent," the translators did not mean to imply that God sins and therefore needs repentance.

Second, the KJV is not consistent in its translation of the Hebrew word וַיִּנָּחֶם as "repent." Elsewhere in Genesis it is translated:

> And Isaac brought her into his mother Sarah's tent, and took Rebekah, and she became his wife; and he loved her: and Isaac *was comforted* after his mother's death (Gen. 24:67).
>
> And in process of time the daughter of Shuah Judah's wife died; and Judah *was comforted*, and went up unto his sheepshearers to Timnath, he and his friend Hirah the Adullamite (Gen. 38:12).

---

[1] Stephen Davis, *Logic and the Nature of God*, (Grand Rapids, Mich; Eerdmans, 1983) ppg 88, 96.

> Now therefore fear ye not: I will nourish you, and your little ones. And he *comforted* them, and spake kindly unto them (Gen. 50:21).

Obviously, the word "repent" would not fit into the other places in Genesis where the Hebrew word is found. It is translated "to comfort." This reveals that the Hebrew word is an *emotive* term signifying *a change in feelings or emotion*. Gen. 6:6 is a good example.

> And it repented the LORD that he had made man on the earth, and it grieved him at his heart. (KJV)

וַיִּנָּחֶם יְהוָה כִּי־עָשָׂה אֶת־הָאָדָם בָּאָרֶץ וַיִּתְעַצֵּב אֶל־לִבּוֹ׃

Modern translations render the word וַיִּנָּחֶם as follows:

- RSV: was sorry
- NKJ: was sorry
- NRS: was sorry
- NASB: was sorry
- Moffat: was sorry
- Torah: was saddened
- Taylor: broke his heart

Why have modern translators changed "repented" to such emotive words as "sorry"? There are good reasons for what they did.

First, there is a parallelism in the Hebrew text that indicates what the word וַיִּנָּחֶם means. The parallel word is וַיִּתְעַצֵּב and is correctly translated "was grieved." Thus the word וַיִּנָּחֶם refers to the emotions or attitude of God, not His plans or intellect.

If this is true, then we would expect to find the ancient translations rendering the Hebrew word וַיִּנָּחֶם as an emotive term.

- The Septuagint: angry (ἐνεθυμήθη possibly from θυμόω)
- Targum Neofiti 1: regret
- Targun Pseudo-Jonathan: regret
- Syriac: grieve
- Arabic: grieve
- Latin Vulgate: regret (paenituit)

Keil and Delitzsch's comment on Gen. 6:6 is worth repeating.

> The force of יִנָּחֶם "it *repented* the Lord," may be gathered from the explanatory יִתְעַצֵּב, "it grieved Him at his heart." This shows that the repentance of God does not presuppose any variableness in His nature or His purpose, In this sense God never repents of anything (1 Sam. Xv..29), "quia nihil illi inopinatum vel non praevisum accidit" (Calvin). The repentance of God is an anthropomorphic expression for the pain of the divine love at the sin of man, and signifies that "God is hurt no less by the atrocious sins of men than if

they pierced His heart with mortal anguish" (Calvin).[2]

If the authors of Scripture believed that "x" will *certainly* happen in the future, they would express that idea by saying that "x" *shall* or *will* happen. They would have to use "shall" and "will" because they are part of the *language of certitude.* They could strengthen that idea by saying that "x" shall or will *surely* or *certainly* happen in the future.

If they went one step further and used *the language of necessity*, they would say that "x" *must* happen in the future. Thus if "x" *shall* and *must* happen in the future, then future events are both *certain* and *necessary.*

If they believed that the future events are neither certain nor necessary, they would avoid using such language as "shall," "will" and "must." To say that they used the language of certitude and necessity but did not believe in either is make them into fools or liars.

Does the Future Change?

Some humanistic theologians have attempted to find passages in the Bible where they claim that man changed the future. If man can change the future, then the future is not already decided by God. Instead, it is open to contingency (luck and chance) and closed to Divine determinism. Why someone would choose to believe that the universe is open to Lady Luck but closed to the Lord is beyond us.

One such passage is 1 Sam. 23:6-13. The story is quite simple. David had fled to the city of Keilah. When David

---

[2] Keil and Delitzsch, ibid., Genesis I:139-140. See also Gleason Archer, *Encyclopedia of Bible Difficulties*, (Grand Rapids, Mich.; Zondervan, 1982) ppg 80-81.

found out that Saul was planing to march to Keilah, he sought the Lord for guidance. Should he go or stay at Keilah? If he stayed at Keilah, would the men of Keilah turn him over to Saul? The Lord said that if he stayed, they would betray David. Thus he fled the city and escaped Saul.

When God told David that if he stayed at Keilah, he would die, does this mean that God had *predicted* that this would happen? Some humanistic theologians say, "Yes, God had planned that David would in fact die at Keilah. But, when David ran away, he changed the future. His escape changed God's plans and decrees." There are several errors at the core of the humanist argument.

First, in the context, the subjects of God's knowledge, His eternal plans or decrees, and the nature of future events is not addressed. The passage has to do with *personal guidance* in the light of future possibilities from the standpoint of man. Thus this is not a primary passage but a secondary text.

Second, in terms of literary genre, 1 Sam 23 is a historical narrative. A first year seminary student knows that it is hermeneutically precarious to establish a doctrine on historical narratives.

Third, when we think about the future, all we can do is *imagine the possibilities from our viewpoint* because we do not know the actualities of what will in fact happen. But God is not so limited. He knows the actualities as well as all the possibilities because He knows, and has always known, what will take place from the beginning of time to the end.

Since man does not know what the future holds, he can only know the future in terms of what can *possibly* happen according to his understanding. He does not know future actualities. Therefore, the future is "open" to man in the sense that he can imagine many different future possibilities.

The humanists make the fatal error of assuming that God is limited like man when it comes to the future.

The fourth fatal error is that the humanist assumes that *what is possible to man is actual to God.* It is this assumption that controls their interpretation of 1 Sam 23. For example, if I ask God, "Lord, if I stand in front of an oncoming bus and it runs me over, will I die?" If the Lord replies, "Yes, you will die." Does this mean that God was *predicting* that the future *actually* was for me to be run over by a bus, or were my question and His answer *hypothetical scenarios*?

Hypothetical scenarios refer to all the *possible* situations that *I* can *imagine* that could happen, *given the proper circumstances.* If a bus runs over me, given certain hypothetical circumstances, I will die. If David remains at Keilah, given certain hypothetical circumstances, he will die.

The humanist at this point assumes that since my being run over by a bus is a *possible* future event *to me*, this means that God had actually ordained it to happen, that when I chose not to get run over by that bus, I changed the future and then God had to change His eternal decree.

The fifth reason is interesting. When the humanists bring up this passage, they always neglect to quote 1 Sam 23:14 which says,

> And David abode in the wilderness in the strongholds, and remained in the hill-country in the wilderness of Ziph. And Saul sought him every day, but *God did not deliver him into his hand.*

The reason that Saul at Keilah or anywhere else did not kill David was not due to David changing the future but to *the intervention of a Sovereign God.*

Lastly, this passage does not refute the omniscience of God but rather establishes it. The only grounds on which David could ask God about possible future scenarios is that he assumed that God knew all things.

Is the Future Open to Infinite Possibilities?

Is it possible for God to lie? For God to make a mistake? To break His promise? Is it possible that in the future God could become the devil and the devil become God? Can the devil win in the end? The humanist, given his worldview, must believe that all these things are possible. Anyone who says that the future is open to infinite possible worlds, would have to go down the same path of apostasy as Stephen Davis and Clark Pinnock.

According to the biblical worldview, it is *impossible* for God to lie (Tit. 1:3). God cannot fail to keep His word (Num. 23:19). He *cannot* deny His own nature (2 Tim. 2:13).The Lord will win, not the devil (Rev. 20:10). *The impossibility of God becoming the devil or lying is only possible because the future is NOT open to contingency (luck and chance). Only in a predetermined universe can we say that some things are NOT possible.*

Figurative Language

We have no problem handling these secondary texts because Scripture sometimes speaks to us in "figurative language" (John 16:25). Paul tells us that he spoke "in human terms" (Rom. 3:5). Why? "I am speaking in human terms because of the weakness of your flesh" (Rom. 6:19). Thus he did not hesitate to "speak in terms of human relationships" (Gal. 3:15).

This is not a "cop out." Orthodox theologians have biblical precedent to interpret these secondary texts as the use of the *figurative language of human terminology*. Because we would have to go to Sodom to see if it were as bad as we have heard, God is pictured in this figurative sense as doing so.

Changes In Revelation

We must also point out that a *change in special revelation* in which God commands someone to do something and then, from our perspective, "changes His mind" and tells him not to do it, does not biblically imply any change in the eternal plans of God. He sometimes tests the hearts of men so that *they* might know where they are spiritually.

For example, when God commanded Abraham to kill Isaac, this does not mean that He had ordained that Isaac would die by his father's knife. Thus God had a ram going up the one side of the same mountain while Abraham and Isaac went up the other. The ram was already provided as the substitute sacirifice because God NEVER intended His command to be carried out. He wanted Abraham to know that God must have first place in his life, not Isaac.

When God *revealed* to Moses, "I am going to destroy Israel," and then Moses offered to die instead, from the perspective of man, it would appear that God changed His mind and decided not to destroy Israel (Exo. 32:10f). But God never intended to destroy the Jewish people because He had already predicted the coming of the Messiah. God was not going to invalidate hundreds of messanic prophecies by wiping out the Jewish people. *A change in revelation does not imply a change in God's mind or eternal decrees.*

The same point can be made about God's threat to destroy Ninevah (Jonah 3). They repented under the *preaching* of the prophet (Matt. 12:41). Today we preach, "Turn or burn! Repent or perish!" This does not mean that God has decreed us to burn and perish but rather that if we do not repent, that will be our doom.

Conclusion

The God who is there is not silent about the fact and nature of His knowledge of Himself and the world He created. Philosophers may question or even deny revealed truth but they cannot overthrow it.

PART III

THE EXTENT OF GOD'S KNOWLEDGE

Did the authors of Scripture believe that God's knowledge was infinite in its extent and that nothing was closed to the knowledge of God? How would they convey this idea to their readers? By what vocabulary?

Given these questions, we would expect to find them using the same general format they followed when teaching any revealed truth. They usually give us *general statements* which directly teach the truth and then they give us *specific* illustrations of it.

GENERAL STATEMENTS ABOUT THE EXTENT OF GOD'S KNOWLEDGE

Does the Bible state specifically and directly that God knows *everything*? Is this the understanding of the authors of Scripture? If they believed that God did *not* know everything, then we would expect them to state this in a clear manner. Let us turn to the Word of God for our answer.

HANNAH'S CONFESSION OF FAITH

We have already seen that Hannah's use of the plural דֵּעוֹת indicates that Yahweh is the God of all knowledge, whatever kind it is.

> The LORD is a God of knowledge (1 Sam. 2:3)

When someone says, "The knowledge of the future is a kind of knowledge that God cannot know," he is violating Hannah's clear confession of faith.

PSALM 139

Psalm 139 is a passage of full mention on the extent of God's knowledge. David says to Yahweh, "You know everything" (v. 4). Then he lists all the things that God knows including his future thoughts and words before they even enter his mind.

> v. 1, O LORD, You have *searched me* and *known me.*
>
> לַמְנַצֵּחַ לְדָוִד מִזְמוֹר יְהוָה חֲקַרְתַּנִי וַתֵּדָע׃
>
> κύριε ἐδοκίμασάς με καὶ ἔγνως με
>
> v. 2, You *know* when I sit down and when I rise up; You *understand* my thoughts from afar.
>
> אַתָּה יָדַעְתָּ שִׁבְתִּי וְקוּמִי בַּנְתָּה לְרֵעִי מֵרָחוֹק׃
>
> σὺ ἔγνως τὴν καθέδραν μου καὶ τὴν ἔγερσίν μου σὺ συνῆκας τοὺς διαλογισμούς μου ἀπὸ μακρόθεν
>
> v. 3, You *scrutinize* my path and my lying down.

אָרְחִי וְרִבְעִי זֵרִיתָ וְכָל־דְּרָכַי הִסְכַּנְתָּה׃

τὴν τρίβον μου καὶ τὴν σχοῖνόν μου σὺ ἐξιχνίασας
καὶ πάσας τὰς ὁδούς μου προεῖδες

v. 4, Even before there is a word on my tongue, Behold, O LORD, *You know everything.*

אֵין מִלָּה בִּלְשׁוֹנִי הֵן יְהוָה יָדַעְתָּ כֻלָּהּ׃
כִּי

ὅτι οὐκ ἔστιν λόγος ἐν γλώσσῃ μου

ἰδού κύριε σὺ ἔγνως πάντα τὰ ἔσχατα

v. 5, You have enclosed me behind and before, and laid Your hand upon me.

אחוֹר וָקֶדֶם צַרְתָּנִי וַתָּשֶׁת עָלַי כַּפֶּכָה׃

καὶ τὰ ἀρχαῖα σὺ ἔπλασάς με καὶ ἔθηκας
ἐπ᾽ ἐμὲ τὴν χεῖρά σου

v. 6, Such knowledge is too wonderful for me;

It is too high, I cannot attain to it.

דַעַת מִמֶּנִּי נִשְׂגְּבָה לֹא־אוּכַל לָהּ׃
(פְּלִאִיָּה) [פְּלִיאָה]

ἐθαυμαστώθη ἡ γνῶσίς σου ἐξ ἐμοῦ
ἐκραταιώθη οὐ μὴ δύνωμαι πρὸς αὐτήν

The Psalmist uses every word and phrase in the Hebrew language to indicate the infinite extent of God's knowledge. The passage above is so clear and distinct on the infinite extent of God's knowledge that we have never seen any attempt by those who limit God's knowledge to explain it away. They simply ignore it and proceed with their philosophic speculations.

IS GOD'S UNDERSTANDING INFINITE?

Instead of sitting around and pooling our ignorance on the subject, what has God revealed about this question in Scripture?

> Great is our Lord, and mighty in power;
>
> *His understanding is infinite* (Psa. 147:5).
>
> גָּדוֹל אֲדוֹנֵינוּ וְרַב־כֹּחַ לִתְבוּנָתוֹ אֵין מִסְפָּר׃
>
> μέγας ὁ κύριος ἡμῶν καὶ μεγάλη ἡ ἰσχὺς αὐτοῦ καὶ τῆς συνέσεως <u>αὐτοῦ οὐκ ἔστιν ἀριθμός</u>

In the context, God's glory is revealed by His omniscience because,

> He counteth the number of the stars; He calls
>
> them all by *their* names.
>
> מוֹנֶה מִסְפָּר לַכּוֹכָבִים לְכֻלָּם שֵׁמוֹת יִקְרָא׃
>
> ὁ ἀριθμῶν πλήθη ἄστρων καὶ πᾶσιν αὐτοῖς ὀνόματα καλῶν

The universe may be vast and immeasurable to man but it is only a finite speck of dust to the Almighty. He knows its measurements because He made it.

In v. 5, the Psalmist gives a poetic contrast between the finite universe and the infinite nature of God. Yahweh is "great" (Heb. גדול Gk. μέγας). He is a "mega" God, and not some finite deity like the heathen worship.

God is "great" for two reasons:

a. He is *omnipotent in power* because He is "abundant in strength." His power has no limits. There is nothing that is beyond the power of God to accomplish.

b. He is *omniscient in knowledge* because, as Leupold correctly translates the Hebrew phrase, "There is no limit to His understanding."[1]

The words in v.5, אֵין מִסְפָּר, mean that God's "knowledge" or "understanding" cannot be numerically quantified as the stars can. There is no number which can represent God's knowledge because it is infinite in nature; hence, there is no limit to it or on it. The classic commentator Delitzsch points out,

> To His understanding there is no number; i.e., in its depth and fullness it cannot be defined by any number. What a comfort for the church as it traverses it ways, that are often so labyrinthine and entangled! Its Lord is the Omniscient as well as the Almighty One.[2]

---

[1] H. H. Leupold, Exposition of the Psalms, (Grand Rapids, Mich.; Baker Book House, 1959), pg. 989.

[2] Frans Delitzsch, *Biblical Commentary on the Psalms*, (Grand Rapids, Mich.; Eerdmans, n.d.) vol. 3, pg. 400.

In his commentary on the Psalms, Moll states,

> He has assigned a number to the stars which men cannot count (Gen. XV.5). This means that, in creating them, He called forth a number determined by Himself. It is also said that He calls them all by name; i.e., that He knows and names them according to their special features, and employs them in His service according to His will, in conformity with the names which correspond to such knowledge. The Omniscience and Omnipotence of God are thus presented at once to the soul. The greatness of God (v.5) with respect to might (Job XXXVII.23) corresponds to the fullness of His understanding (Psa. CXLV.3), which no number can express. The same Lord who, with infinite power and unsearchable wisdom, rules the stars in their courses, rules also the world of man.[3]

The prophet Isaiah followed the Psalmist in using the same word לִתְבוּנָתוֹ for God's "understanding" when he declared,

> Have you not known? Have you not heard? The everlasting God, Jehovah, the Creator of the ends of the earth, fainteth not, neither is weary; *there is no searching out of his understanding.* (Isaiah 40:28)

---

[3] Carl Moll, *The Psalms*, found in *Lange's Commentary on the Holy Scripture*, (Grand Rapids, Mich.; Zondervan, n.d.) vol. 9, pg. 671.

יָדַעְתָּ אִם־לֹא שָׁמַעְתָּ אֱלֹהֵי עוֹלָם
קְצוֹת הָאָרֶץ לֹא יִיעַף וְלֹא הֲלוֹא
יִיגָע אֵין חֵקֶר לִתְבוּנָתוֹ: יְהוָה בּוֹרֵא

The Septuagint is emphatic in its translation. It uses the word φρονήσεως as the Greek equivalent for the Hebrew לִתְבוּנָתוֹ. Thus the translators were stressing that God's way of thinking; i.e., *how* He knows all things, is incomprehensible to man.

> καὶ νῦν οὐκ ἔγνως εἰ μὴ ἤκουσας θεὸς αἰώνιος ὁ θεὸς ὁ κατασκευάσας τὰ ἄκρα τῆς γῆς οὐ πεινάσει οὐδὲ κοπιάσει <u>οὐδὲ ἔστιν ἐξεύρεσις τῆς φρονήσεως αὐτοῦ</u>

The Apostle John declared his understanding of the extent of God's knowledge in language that is hard to dismiss.

> If our hearts condemn us, God is greater than our hearts and *knows everything* (1 John 3:20).

> ὅτι ἐὰν καταγινώσκῃ ἡμῶν ἡ καρδία, ὅτι μείζων ἐστὶν ὁ θεὸς τῆς καρδίας ἡμῶν καὶ <u>γινώσκει πάντα.</u>

In the context, John follows David in describing God as the "mega God" because He is greater (μείζων) than us; i.e., He is omnipotent. Then he adds that not only is God greater in power than we are, but He is also greater in knowledge because He knows all things. There is nothing in the context to indicate that we should limit "everything."

The author of Hebrews is picturesque as well as transparent in his view of the extent of God's knowledge.

> No creature can hide from him. Everything is naked and helpless before the eyes of the one to whom we must give an account (Heb. 4:13).
>
> καὶ οὐκ ἔστιν κτίσις ἀφανὴς ἐνώπιον αὐτοῦ, πάντα δὲ γυμνὰ καὶ τετραχηλισμένα τοῖς ὀφθαλμοῖς αὐτοῦ, πρὸς ὃν ἡμῖν ὁ λόγος.

The author of Hebrews speaks of God's knowledge first in the negative and then in the positive. He first says that there is nothing in the universe that is closed to God's sight. There is no creature great or small, *not even man*, that escapes the omniscient eye of the Creator.

Second, "all things" are open to God's sight. How else could God "work all things together" for our good and His glory (Rom. 8:28)? How could He be "working all things after the counsel of His will" (Eph. 1:11) if He did not know what was going to happen next? This passage is so comprehensive and all encompassing, that we cannot limit the Mind of God in any sense. How then can some claim that the future is *closed* to His sight?

AN OMNISCIENT MESSIAH

The divine nature of the God/man at times revealed itself while He was on earth. In the following places the divine attribute of omniscience was applied to Him.

> But Jesus did not trust himself unto them, because *He knew all things* (John 2:24).
>
> αὐτὸς δὲ Ἰησοῦς οὐκ ἐπίστευεν αὐτὸν αὐτοῖς διὰ τὸ αὐτὸν γινώσκειν πάντας

Note the use of the infinitive γινώσκειν. The divine nature of the Messiah was at all times omniscient.

> ...and *didn't need anyone to tell him what people were like. For he himself knew what was in every person* (John 2:25).
>
> καὶ ὅτι οὐ χρείαν εἶχεν ἵνα τις μαρτυρήσῃ περὶ τοῦ ἀνθρώπου· αὐτὸς γὰρ ἐγίνωσκεν τί ἦν ἐν τῷ ἀνθρώπῳ.

We must remember that John is writing after Christ ascended to heaven. The ascended Messiah knows the spiritual condition of the hearts of all men because He is omniscient. In Rev. 2:23, the ascended Christ says,

> I am the one who searches minds and hearts. I will reward each one of you as your works deserve.
>
> ἐγώ εἰμι ὁ ἐραυνῶν νεφροὺς καὶ καρδίας, καὶ δώσω ὑμῖν ἑκάστῳ κατὰ τὰ ἔργα ὑμῶν.

Christ uses the same phraseology found in the Old Testament where it describes the omniscience of Yahweh (Psa. 7:9; Jer. 11:20, 17:10).

> Now we know that *you know everything* and do not need to have anyone to ask you questions. Because of this, we believe that you have come from God (John 16:30).
>
> νῦν οἴδαμεν ὅτι οἶδας πάντα καὶ οὐ χρείαν ἔχεις ἵνα τίς σε ἐρωτᾷ· ἐν τούτῳ πιστεύομεν ὅτι ἀπὸ θεοῦ ἐξῆλθες.

In the context, the disciples had come to realize that Jesus was not simply a man with limited human knowledge like themselves. But Jesus was God as well as man and thus He was omniscient in His divine nature (John 20:28).

> He said to him a third time, "Simon, son of John, do you love me?" And Peter was deeply hurt that he had said to him a third time, "Do you love me?" So he said to him, "Lord, *You know everything.* You know that I love you!" (John 21: 17).

> λέγει αὐτῷ τὸ τρίτον, Σίμων Ἰωάννου, φιλεῖς με; ἐλυπήθη ὁ Πέτρος ὅτι εἶπεν αὐτῷ τὸ τρίτον, Φιλεῖς με; καὶ λέγει αὐτῷ, Κύριε, πάντα σὺ οἶδας, σὺ γινώσκεις ὅτι φιλῶ σε. λέγει αὐτῷ [ὁ Ἰησοῦς], Βόσκε τὰ πρόβατά μου.

Peter inverts the normal word order by putting the word πάντα ("all") first to emphasize that Christ knows ALL in an absolute sense. There is no way in the context to escape the truth of Peter's confession. Jesus the Christ, the Son of the living God, Second Person of the Holy Trinity, knows ALL things.

SPECIFIC ILLUSTRATIONS

GOD'S KNOWLEDGE OF HIMSELF

- His eternal plans for man and the universe: 2 Kings 19:25; Jer. 29:11-12; Acts 1:7.
- His future works are known to Him from eternity: Acts 15:18.
- Exhaustive knowledge of each member of the Trinity of the other members of the Godhead: Mat. 11:27; John 7:29, 8:55, 17:25; 1 Cor. 2:10-11.

GOD'S KNOWLEDGE OF THE SPACE/TIME UNIVERSE

- All of history, the end from the beginning: Isa. 46:10.
- Extends to the ends of the earth: Job 28:24.
- Sees everything under the heavens: Job 28:24.
- All possible events in the future: Isa. 48:18-19; Ezk. 37:3; Mat. 11:21-23.
- When a sparrow falls to the ground: Mat. 10:29.
- He speaks of future events as if they already happened: Rom. 4:17; 8:30.
- The number and names of the stars: Psa. 147:4.
- All creatures: Heb. 4:13.
- When He will judge the world: Mat. 8:29; Acts 17:31; Rev. 14:7,15.
- He foresees the future: Gal. 3:8-9.
- He foreknows the future: Acts 2:23; Rom. 8:29; 1 Pet. 1:2, 18-20.

GOD'S KNOWLEDGE OF MAN

- All men: 2 Sam. 7:20; Psa. 33:13; Jer. 15:15.
- The hearts of all men: 1 Sam. 16:7; 1 Kings 8:39: Psa. 7:9; 17:2; 26:2; 139:2; Jer. 11:20; 12:3; 17:10; Lk. 16:15; John 2:24; 21:17; Acts 1:24; Rom. 8:27; Rev. 2:23.
- When a man will be born and when he will die: Job 14:5: 21:21; Psa. 31:15; Mat. 26:18,

45; Mk. 14:35,41; John 2:4; 7:6,8,30; 8:30; 12:27; 13:1; Acts 17:26.

- Man's ways: Job 23:10; 34:21.
- Man's thoughts: Psa. 139:2; Ezk. 11:5; Heb. 4:12.
- Man's meditations: Psa. 5:1.
- Man's works: Job 34:25; Psa. 33:15; Matt. 16:27.
- Man's sorrows: Gen. 29:32; 31:42; Exo. 3:7; 4:31; Psa. 25:18-19; 31:7; 119:153.
- Every word man speaks: Jer. 17:16.
- A man's future: Exo. 3:19-20; Jer. 18:22-23.
- How many hairs are on his head: Matt. 10:30.
- The folly of man: Psa. 69:5.
- The wrongs of man: Psa. 69:5.
- The wickedness of man: Gen. 6:5.
- Our future needs and prayers before we ask: Mat. 6:8.
- Every intent of the thoughts of man's heart: Gen. 6:5; Heb. 4:12.
- The shame of man: Psa. 69:19.
- What man is made of: Psa. 103:14.
- Man's actions: Psa. 139:2-4.
- All about a man before he is born: Jer. 1:5.

What about the future acts of man, good and evil? Does God know the future decisions and acts that we will do? The Scripture illustrates that God knows the good and evil that we will do from all eternity and even declares it in prophecy. The following is but a few samples of the *hundreds* of passages in which God reveals what men will think, say and do in the future:

- That in the future, all the evil things that Joseph's brothers, Potiphar's wife and others would do to him would place him where he could save his family from starvation: Gen. 50:20.
- That in the future, Pharaoh would not obey Moses: Exo. 7:3-5.
- That in the future, Nebuchadnezzar would destroy Tyre: Ezek. 26:1-14.
- That in the future, Nebuchadnezzar would conquer Egypt: Ezk. 30:10.
- That in the future, Nebuchadnezzar would conquer Judah: Jer. 25:9.
- That in the future, Judah's captivity would last seventy years: Jer. 25:11.
- That in the future, Babylon would fall in seventy years: Jer. 25:12.
- That in the future, Cyrus would rebuild Jerusalem: Isa. 44:28-45:1.
- That in the future, Judas would betray Jesus: Psa. 41:9; Lk. 22:21-22; John 6:64; 13:18,19,21,26,27.
- That in the future, Peter would deny Him three times: Mat. 26:34.

- That in the future, the Jews, the Romans, Herod, and Pontius Pilate would murder Jesus: Acts 4:27-28.

CONCLUSION

We have examined in some detail what the authors of Scripture said about the nature and extent of God's knowledge. We found them saying what they would have to say in order to convey the idea that God's omniscience is absolute and unlimited by anything past, present or future.

Those who disagree have a great task set before them. If the authors of Scripture believed that God did NOT know the past, present or future, how would they express that idea to their readers? By what vocabulary? By what illustrations?

They will have to come up with multiple biblical passages that clearly state, "He does NOT know everything" or, "I the Lord do NOT know." Let them follow the same procedure as we have followed and marshal their exegetical evidence. They will have to produce primary passages in which the knowledge of God is clearly in focus and that knowledge is specifically limited. Let us now turn to those who deny the omniscience of God.

PART IV

FALSE VIEWS

There are so many clear biblical passages on the perfection of God's knowledge that one wonders how anyone who had ever read the Bible could come up with the ideas that God does not know everything, that His knowledge is dependent upon something outside of Himself, that He is learning new things every second or that His knowledge does not effectually cause whatsoever comes to pass. Jonathan Edwards, the greatest intellect that America ever produced, comments.

> One would think it wholly needless to enter on such an argument with any that profess themselves Christians: but so it is; God's certain Foreknowledge of the free acts of moral agents, is denied by some that pretend to believe the Scriptures to be the Word of God.[1]

There are three clear tests of any view of the nature and extent of God's knowledge.

1. Does this view strengthen or weaken the biblical and evangelical doctrine of the verbal, plenary, inerrant, infallible inspiration of the Bible?
2. Does this view strengthen or weaken the biblical and evangelical doctrine of the substitutionay blood atonement of Christ on the cross?

---

[1] *The Works of Jonathan Edwards* (Edinburgh: Banner of Truth, 1974) vol. I:30.

3. Does this view strengthen or weaken the biblical and evangelical doctrine of Divine Providence over all things?

While there are many other test doctrines that could also be applied to this subject, these three are sufficient to doom any heretical or deviant view. Why? Any view of God which destroys His Word, casts doubt on Christ's atonement and rebels against Divine Providence cannot be of God but comes from Satan.

If these strong words upset you, maybe you have not read your Bible lately. The words of the prophets, the apostles and even our Lord Himself were often far stronger than what we just said. Biblical Christianity is for the tough-minded and does not pussy-foot around with heresy.

All the false views listed below fail the three tests listed above. For example, in the book, *Battle of the Gods,* you will find nearly 300 pages refuting pagan finite godism, process theology and philosophy, neo-processian views and "moral government" theology. Since each of the false views listed below should receive a detailed refutation and this far exceeds the limits of this syllabus, we can only summarize in brief the chief problems with each view. See the resource guide at the end of the syllabus for further study.

THE HISTORY OF FALSE VIEWS

THE ANCIENT POLYTHEISTIC WORLD

The ancient pagans did not believe in one infinite/personal God who was Maker of heaven and earth. Instead, they believed that the universe was eternal and that there were multiple gods and goddesses who were finite; i.e., limited in nature, power and knowledge.

In this pagan worldview, the gods fought among themselves for preeminence. There was no concept of the universe being ruled by one sovereign, infinite God who filled heaven and earth. The chaos of the gods allowed a certain view of man's powers and abilities to develop.

The pagan worldview taught that man was *autonomous* in an absolute sense. He was totally and absolutely "free" and even the gods could not violate this freedom. The Greek philosphers were the first to articulate the idea that man had a "free will" and that no one, not even a god, could violate it. The Greek philospher Epictetus wrote,

> Not even Zeus himself can get the better of my free will.[2]
>
> Who can any longer restrain or compel me, contrary to my own opinion? No more than Zeus.[3]

In a contingent (i.e., chance-driven) universe in which no one was in control, not even the gods, man was totally free to be or do whatever he wanted. Man was even free to become a god if he so chose. Nothing was beyond the ability of man.

The pagan philosophers claimed that man had to be "free" in order for man to be responsible for his actions. If his choices and actions were in any way the result of what other people or even the gods themselves decided, then man was not really free.

---

[2] *Moral Discources of Epictetus*, ed. By Thomas Gould, (New York:Washington Square Press, 1964), p. 7.

[3] ibid, p. 233.

The Greek philosophers demanded that man must be autonomous in order for man to be responsible because they assumed that *man was the measure of all things — including his responsibility.* They understood the word "responsibility" to mean response-ability. Man's responsibility was thus limited by two things: ignorance and inability.

a. If he did not know about something, then he could not be held responsible for doing it.

b. If he did not have the power to do something, he could not be held responsible for not doing it.

There was no concept in the pagan worldview that man's responsibility meant *accountability to his Creator who would one day judge him.* Thus the pagan concept of man's autonomous "free will" was possible only in the context of that pagan polytheistic worldview. [4]

ATHENS VERSUS JERUSALEM

When pagans first became Christians, some of them retained much of their pagan worldview. It was not long before they realized that the biblical worldview did not have room for the pagan concept of man's absolute free will. The choice they faced was whether they should abandon or modify the biblical worldview to make room for the pagan concept of man's freedom or should they abandon the pagan concept of man and submit to revealed truth? The rest of church history is the story of those who tried to mix the oil of the biblical worldview with the water of the pagan worldview and those who saw that such an attempt was useless. In the

---

[4] This point is documented by Royce Gruenler in his chapter in Nash's, *On Process Theolgy* (Grand Rapids, Mich.; Baker, 1987) ppg 330-356.

end, just as the oil and the water will separate, any attempt to marry Christ with Baal will fail.

The biblical authors did not buy into the pagan polytheistic worldview or its doctrine of human autonomy. They taught that man was created by God to bear His image. Therefore human responsibility meant that man was *accountable* to God for whatever God told him to know, be or do. *God was the measure of man's accountability. Man's ignorance and inabilty had no bearing on the issue.*

WHAT ABOUT THE HEATHEN?

Humanistic evangelical philosophers such as Pinnock and Sanders do not believe that the heathen will go to hell. They argue that that if someone has never heard the gospel, he cannot believe. Thus his ignorance and inability are valid *excuses* why God should not condemn him to hell. We have given a full refutation to this view elsewhere and can only summarize it here.[5]

First, as to whether or not the heathen have an excuse, the Apostle Paul in Romans 1:20 states that they are "*without excuse.*" In case he was not understood, he repeated the dramatic words "*without excuse*" in Romans 2:1.

Humanistic theologians and philosophers will present all kinds of *excuses* why the heathen should not be thrown into hell. When we point them to clear Scripture that says that they are "without excuse," they usually repsond, "But...they do have good excuses." It does not seem to dawn on them that they have directly contradicted the Word of God.

---

[5] Robert Morey, *Death and the Afterlife* (Minn: Bethany House Publishers, 1984), ppg 246-256.

Second, they are operating on a false definition of human responsibility. They are assuming the pagan worldview in which man is the measure of all things — including his responsibility. To the extent that man knows and is capable, to that extent he is responsible. But the biblical worldview teaches that man is responsible in the sense that he is *accountable* to an Authority and Power higher than himself.

> For all of us must appear before the judgment-seat of Christ, so that *each one may give an acount* of the things *done* in the body, according to what he has done, whether *it be* good or evil (2 Cor. 5:10).
>
> τοὺς γὰρ πάντας ἡμᾶς φανερωθῆναι δεῖ ἔμπροσθεν τοῦ βήματος τοῦ Χριστοῦ, ἵνα κομίσηται ἕκαστος τὰ διὰ τοῦ σώματος πρὸς ἃ ἔπραξεν, εἴτε ἀγαθὸν εἴτε φαῦλον.

> No creature can hide from him. Everything is naked and helpless before *the eyes of the one to whom we must give an account* (Heb. 4:13).
>
> καὶ οὐκ ἔστιν κτίσις ἀφανὴς ἐνώπιον αὐτοῦ, πάντα δὲ γυμνὰ καὶ τετραχηλισμένα τοῖς ὀφθαλμοῖς αὐτοῦ, πρὸς ὃν ἡμῖν ὁ λόγος.

One way to spot a humanistic thinker is to ask, "Is human responsibility defined in terms of man's ability and knowledge or is it defined in terms of one's accountability to his Creator?" When someone says that man's ability and knowledge limit his responsibility, you are talking with a humanist. If he or she says that man's responsibility is defined by accountability to God, you are dealing with a biblical theist. On the Day of Judgment, man will not be seated on the throne judging God but God will judge every thought, word and deed of man.

IGNORANCE IS NO EXCUSE

In the biblical worldview, man fell into ignorance through sin at the Fall of Adam. Thus ignorance of one's duty to God and man is no excuse before God. This is why in Lev. 4 and Num. 15, if you sinned *in ignorance*, it was still viewed as a sin by God and you still had to offer a sacrifice to atone for that sin. Indeed, Christ will return one day,

> In flaming fire taking vengeance on *those who do not know God* (2 Thess. 1:8).
>
> ἐν πυρὶ φλογός, διδόντος ἐκδίκησιν τοῖς μὴ εἰδόσιν θεὸν

On the Day of Judgment, people will be held accountable to God for what they did not know and for what they did know but disobeyed. They are sometimes called sins of ommission and sins of commission. This is why the heathen go to hell even though they did not know the gospel. Their ignorance does not negate their accountability to God (Psa. 9:17). Paul put it this way,

> For all who have sinned apart from the Law will also perish apart from the Law: and all who have sinned under the Law will be judged by the Law (Rom. 2:12).
>
> ὅσοι γὰρ ἀνόμως ἥμαρτον, ἀνόμως καὶ ἀπολοῦνται, καὶ ὅσοι ἐν νόμῳ ἥμαρτον, διὰ νόμου κριθήσονται·

It does not matter if you had or did not have the teaching of the law of God, if you sin, you will perish. Those who sinned without having a Bible will perish as certainly as those who had a Bible and failed to obey it.

INABILITY IS NO EXCUSE

In the biblical worldview, man fell into spiritual inability through sin at the Fall of Adam. Although man is now a sinner, he still has the responsibility to be as holy and perfect as God (Matt. 5:48; 1 Pet. 1:16). In the following texts, notice the *vocabulary of inability* used by the authors of Scripture:

> No man *can* come to me unless the Father who sent me draws him (John 6:44).
>
> So he said, "This is why I told you that no man *can* come to me unless it be granted him by the Father (John 6:65).
>
> That's why the mind that is set on the flesh is hostile toward God. It refuses to submit to the authority of God's Law because *it is powerless to do so* (Rom. 8:7).
>
> Those who are under the control of the flesh *can't* please God (Rom. 8:8).
>
> A person who isn't spiritual doesn't accept the things of God's Spirit, for they are nonsense to him. *He can't understand them because they are spiritually evaluated* (1 Cor. 2:14).
>
> No man *can* say, "Jesus is Lord," except by the Holy Spirit (1 Cor. 12:3).

Just because *you are not free* to come to Christ, submit to God's Law, confess Christ as Lord or live a perfect and sinless life because *your will is powerless*, does not mean that you will not be held accountable to God. It is because of sin that you are not able to do these things.

BIBLICAL HISTORY

Lastly, if we go through biblical history and look to see if ignorance or inability ever let anyone "off the hook" before God, we find that this *never* happened. Were there ignorant people at the Flood, the Tower of Babel, Sodom and Gomorrah, the conquest of Canaan, the Exodus and the Exiles? Yes. Did their ignorance or inability qualify them to escape the judgment of God? No. Did not Jesus say that the Judgment Day will be like those events? Yes. "As it was in the days of…so shall it be…." *Then ignorance and inability are not valid excuses before God.*

When a humanist responds, "But my god would not condemn ignorant people," respond back to them, "You are right! *Your god* would not do that. But this is the real problem. You have created a false god in your own image. Since *you* would not condemn the heathen, neither can your god. You are assuming that man is the measure of all things, including God."

THE CLASH OF WORLDVIEWS

Francis Schaeffer used to point out that there is room in the biblical worldview for only *one* absolute free will.[6] Imagine that you were shipwrecked on a deserted island. Since no other person was on the island, you had absolute freedom to do what you wanted to do because there was no

---

[6] We cover this issue in greater detail in our syllabus, *The Nature and Extent of Human Freedom* (Faith Defenders, P.O. Box 7447, Orange CA, 92863; 1999). Therefore, we will not go into a detailed discussion of this issue at this time.

one to interfere with that freedom. You did not need to wear clothes if you did not want to. You picked any fruit you wanted. You went where you wanted.

But one day, another person was shipwrecked on the island. All of a sudden, you were no longer absolutely free to do as you please. What if he wanted to eat the same fruit that you wanted to eat? What if he wanted you to pick it for him? What if he wanted you to wear clothing? In the end, only one of you can be free.

In the same way, in the biblical worldview, God is the only One with absolute free will.

> But our God is enthroned in the heavens: *He does whatever He pleases* (Psa.115:3).

> And all the inhabitants of the earth are reputed as nothing; and H*e does according to his will* in the army of heaven, and among the inhabitants of the earth; and none can stay his hand, or say unto him, What doest thou? (Dan. 4:35).

DO YOU BELIEVE IN FREE WILL?

A Christian humanist once asked me, "Do you believe in free will?" I replied, "Yes. *God* has an absolute free will to do with you and me as it pleases Him." The humanist was obviously surprised by my answer. He replied, "I don't mean God's free will, I mean *man's* free will."

I then asked, "Shouldn't we first begin with God and then proceed to man? Where does the Bible begin?"

"Oh," said the humanist, "I see your trick. If we begin with God, then He will end up with an absolute free will and man is limited. Well, I refuse to begin with God because *man* must not be limited — not even by God."

"This," I said, "is the real issue. As a biblical theist, I begin where the Bible begins, 'In the beginning *God*' and as a humanist, you begin where pagan philosophy begins: man is the measure of all things."

AN IRRECCONCILIBLE CONFLICT

Many pagan philsophers, such as Jean Paul Sarte[7], see the issues clearly:

> If the biblical worldview is true, then God is the only One with an absolute free will and man is limited by God.
>
> If the pagan worldview is true, then man is the only one with an absolute free will and the gods or god is limited by man.
>
> It is impossible to reconcile the pagan worldview with the biblical worldview.
>
> In the Bible, God is eternal, infinite and unlimited. The universe was created by God and is limited by Him.
>
> In the pagan worldview, the universe is eternal and the gods are finite and thus limited by the universe. Man is unlimited and totally free — even from the gods.
>
> Monotheism and polytheism cannot be reconciled. Neither can the concepts of man which developed out of them.

[7] Jean Paul Sarte, *Being and Nothingness* (New York: Washington Square Press, 1966) pt. 4, ch.1.

> I must choose between the two. It is either the one or the other. There is no middle ground.
>
> If I choose the pagan worldview of human autonomy in which I am absolutely free, then I must deny that the God of the biblical worldview exists. If He exists, I am limited. If He does not exist, then I am free.
>
> If I choose the biblical worldview, then I must submit to the Lordship of Christ over all of life.

While this is understood by many secular philosophers, some "Christian" philosophers and theologians have tried in vain to reconcile the pagan worldview with the biblical worldview. But their attempts have always failed because they always begin as their fundamental starting point with the pagan idea that man has to be totally free and unlimited in the classic Greek philosophic sense of absolute human autonomy. They never begin with God or His revelation. If you begin with man, you will never end with the God of the biblical worldview.

FAILED ATTEMPTS AT SYNERGISM

Throughout church history there have been people who tried to blend together in some kind of synergistic system the pagan worldview of autonomous man with the biblical world view of a Sovereign God. They have always ended in failure because Christ and Satan will never walk together hand in hand. In the end, there can be only one.

> Stop becoming unevenly yoked with unbelievers. What partnership can righteousness have with lawlessness? What

> fellowship can light have with darkness? What harmony exists between Christ with Belial, or what do a believer and an unbeliever have in common? What agreement can a temple of God make with with idols? (2 Cor. 6:14-16).

No one will be able to reconcile two radically different worldviews because we cannot serve two Masters. We will always end up hating one of them and serving the other. Either we choose the sovereign God of the Bible or the autonomous man of pagan philosophy. [8]

GNOSTICS, MANICHAEANS, MARCIONITES, AND VALENTIANS

The heresies which plagued the early Church such as Gnosticism, Manichaeanism, Marcionism and Valentianism all taught that God had to be limited in knowledge and power in order for man to be absolutely free. God could not know the future as this would limit man's freedom. Many of the early Christian creeds where written in such a way as to exclude from the Church those who limited God's knowledge or power.

THE RENAISSANCE

The "Age of Reason" has incorrectly been contrasted to the "Age of Faith." The battle has never been between reason and faith *per se* but between *human reason* and *Divine revelation*. It takes a great deal of faith to believe that man is totally free. It also takes faith to bow before Scripture. Thus the issue is not faith but the Object of our faith: either God or man.

---

[8] See Robert Morey, *Battle of the Gods*, (Faith Defenders, P.O. Box 7447, Orange CA, 92863; 1999), ppg 57-68.

THE SOCINIANS AND UNITARIANS

The *Socinians* not only denied the Trinity and the inspiration of the Bible, they also denied that God knew the future and that God's foreknowledge guaranteed that future events would necessarily happen according to God's decrees.

From the Socinians came the *Unitarians* who claimed that God did not choose to know all of the future. He chose not to know the future free acts of man.

JEHOVAH'S WITNESSES, MORMONS AND OTHER CULTS

The idea that God does not choose to know the future free acts of man was picked up by such Arian cults as the Watchtower and also by polytheistic cults like the LDS Mormons. [9]

The main problem with this argument is that not only is it absolutely unbiblical but it is plainly idiotic. In order for God to choose what future events He wants to know and what future events He does *not* want to know, He has to first know them *all.* If A through Z is going to happen in the future, in order for God to select b, g, l, r, s and t as things He does not want to know, He first has to know them. Otherwise, His knowledge becomes a haphazard, chance-driven, cosmic crap game. To think that God's knowledge is decided by a roll of the dice would not inspire us to worship God!

---

[9] *Aid to Bible Understanding* (Brooklyn: Watchtower Bible & Tract Society, 1971) p. 594f.

See also: Robert Morey, *The Trinity: Evidence and Issues* (Grand Rapids, Mich.; World Publishing, 1996) pgs. 258-261.

PROCESSIANISM

Alfred North Whitehead was one of the most vicious anti-Christians of the 20th century. He claimed that the God of the Bible was his view of the devil and that Christianity with its concept of sin was one of the worse things that ever happened to humanity. Jesus himself was not very intelligent. When asked if he read the Bible, he responded that he preferred Plato.[10]

He taught that God was the soul of the world and the world was God's body. The two were in an eternal bi-polar relationship. You can't have one without the other. God could not know the future because it was open to unlimited possibilities. God was evolving and, in the end, the heavens and the earth would beget God.

With such sheer blasphemy and anti-Christian bigotry, one would not expect anyone to call him a "Christian" theologian and philosopher. But humanistic Christian philosophers and theologians refer to him as a "Christian" thinker whose "insights" are valuable. If you think that we are too severe in our condemnation of Whitehead and the processianism that he invented, Ronald Nash had this to say,

> To its critics, process theology is the most dangerous heresy presently threatening the Christian Faith. Process theology does not eliminate pagan ideas from the faith, its critics argue. Rather, Process thought is a total capitulation to paganism.[11]

---

[10] See *Battle of the Gods*, for documentation on Whitehead.

[11] *On Process Theology*, ed. Ronald Nash (Grand Rapids, Mich.; Baker, 1987). From the Introduction.

> Here there is no middle ground…A being who is not essentially omnipotent or omniscient, who is not the sovereign and independent Creator, is neither worthy to receive our worship nor to bear the title "God."[12]

Some of Whitehead's followers included Charles Hartshorne, Schubert Ogden, David Griffin, Norman Pittenger, H. P. Owen, John Cobb, Jr., Nelson Pike, L. McCabe, and Lewis Ford. They have attacked Christianity and the Bible with great vigor.

No wonder Bruce Demarest concluded,

> A former student of Whitehead reported that the master once commented that Christian orthodoxy could not be reconciled with his philosophy. Moreover, Brown, James, and Reeves acknowledge that process theology bears affinities with Theravada Buddhism, the thought of Heraclitus, the Unitarian Socinus, and the idealist philosophies of Hegel, Schelling, and T. deChardin. By its own admission, then, process theology represents a departure from a theology that broadly could be called biblical and historic Christian.[13]

NEO-PROCESSIANISM IN NEO-EVANGELICAL CIRCLES

In neo-evangelical circles, one finds the heretical theories of Whitehead taught by such people as Clark

---

[12] ibid, p.27.

[13] On Process Theolgy, ibid. p. 78.

Pinnock,[14] Richard Rice,[15] Gregory Boyd,[16] Stephen Davis,[17] Bruce Reichenbach,[18] Gordon Olson,[19] H. Roy Elseth,[20] George Otis, Jr.,[21] and many others.

Neo-processians are absolutely dogmatic that their god *cannot* know the future. But while their god does not know or ordain the future, they think that they and others *can* know the future! Richard Rice is a Seventh Day Adventist and was faced with the rude reality that while he could deny that God knew the future and still keep his job, if he dared to deny that Ellen G. White knew the future, he would soon be collecting unemployment checks. Thus in the first edition of his book, he argued that while God did not know the future, Ellen G. White did!

---

[14] *Predestination & Free Will*, ed. David Basinger & Randall Basinger (Downers Grove IL; IVP, 1986).

[15] Richard Rice, *The Openess of God* (Nashville TN; Review & Herald Pub., 1979).

[16] Gregory Boyd, *Trinity In Process* (New York NY; Peter Lang).

[17] Stephen Davis, *Logic and the Nature of God*, ibid.

[18] *Predestination & Free Will*, ed. David Basinger & Randall Basinger, ibid.

[19] Gordon C. Olson, *The Truth Shall Set You Free* (Franklin Park, Ill: Bible Research Fellowship, 1980).

[20] Howard Roy Elseth, *Did God Know?* (St. Paul, Minn: Calvary United Church, 1977).

[21] George Otis, Jr., "The Foreknowledge of God," unpublished paper, 1941.

Clark Pinnock is quite dogmatic that there is no eternal hell awaiting unbelievers in the future. He is quite sure that the heathen will not end up in hell either. But Pinnock is equally dogmatic that the future is not fixed and God cannot know it. Evidently, while God does not know the future and it is not fixed, Pinnock *knows* there is no future hell awaiting sinners! Evidently, he knows more than his god.

One clue that you are dealing with a humantistic theologian or philospher is whether they recommend any of the theologians listed above. If someone begins to praise the men listed above, run — don't walk — to the nearest exit!

CHRIST DID NOT DIE FOR YOU OR YOUR SINS

What are the implications of process thought? If God does not know the future, did He know that Christ would die? Elseth, Rice and others would say, "No. God did not know that Jesus would die on the cross." Does Jesus know the future? "No, he does not know the future." If God and Jesus do not know the future, particularly the free acts of man such as his sins, then did Jesus know of you and die for your sins when He hung on the tree? "No. God and Jesus did not know of you or your sins because they were in the future."

We have engaged in arguments with processians who deny that Jesus knew of or died for our sins. Yet, they are still running around in evangelical circles claiming to be fellow Christians. Although it is not politically correct today to question people's profession of faith, anyone who denies that Jesus knew me and died for my sins on the cross has denied the Gospel and is under the anathema of God (1 Cor. 15:3-4; Gal. 1:8).

DRIFTING INTO MORMON THEOLOGY

It is interesting to note that when the Mormons responded to Beckwith's book, *The Mormon Concept of God*, they were delighted that he had abandoned the historic orthodox view of omniscience and was moving over to *their* way of thinking. They then applauded Clark Pinnock and his "rat pack" for adopting the Mormon doctrine of the Openness of God! [22] Thus, when we complain that Middle Knowledge and Process theology are doctrines found in the cults and in the occult, we have good reason to say this.

Carl F. Henry, in a powerful chapter entitled, "The Stunted God of Process Theology," sums up why Biblical theists are so hard on process theology.

> Orthodox Christians, both Protestant and Catholic, deplore the way in which process thinkers reject the supernatural, spurn the objective reality of the Trinity, disavow the miraculous, and repudiate a Word of God mediated solely through Christ. They object to the elimination by most process theologians of Christ as the mediator through whom alone God speaks His word. Process theologians also assail the traditional instance on divine decrees and election, on *creatio ex nihilo*, on miraculous redemption and on biblical eschatology. In place of divine decree and foreordination, process thinkers stress

[22] Blake, T. Oster, *Review of Books on the Book of Mormon* 8/2 (1996): 99-146.

> divine persuasion; they subordinate history and eschatological finalities broadly to the endless love of God. So great is the gulf between the two systems of theology that both can hardly lay claim to the title "Christian."[23]

THE COUNTER REFORMATION

The Pope did not sit idly by while half of Europe walked out of his church and into the freedom of the gospel. He launched a counter-Reformation movement whose goal was to recapture those nations and individuals who had become Protestants. The Society of Jesus (or the Jesuits) was given the task of retaking those countries that had been won over by the preaching of the Reformers. They used two methods to overcome Protestantism.[24]

First, they kidnapped, raped, sodomized, tortured, murdered and made war on Protestants to force them to return to popery. The Jesuits, during the Thirty Years War and in the Inquisition, slaughtered several million Protestants. (See *Fox's Book of Martyrs* for the details.)

Second, they invented doctrines that would undercut the four foundational truths of the Reformation: salvation is by *grace alone*, through *faith alone*, in *Christ alone*, according to *Scripture alone.*

According to *all* the standard reference works, a Jesuit priest by the name of Luis de Molina invented the idea that

---

[23] *On Process Theology*, ibid. ppg 362-363.

[24] *The Catholic Encyclopedia* (Nashville TN; Thomas Nelson, 1987) p 396.

God's decisions (i.e., decrees) in eternity are in response to what He foresees us initiating in the future. In this way, Molina could undercut the Reformation doctrines of the absolute necessity and efficacy of God's grace. It is interesting to note that his book on the subject was dedicated to the Inquisition of Portugal where the Jesuits murdered many people.

Does God reward us with the decree of salvation on the basis of what He foresaw we would do by our own power? Thus, He decreed to save us because He foresaw that we would repent and believe? Is God's grace given in response to what we will do before (and thus without) His grace? Does He love us because He foresaw that we would first love Him? Does He choose us because He foresaw that we would first choose Him? Molina's end result is that God's decree to save us is a *reward* for what God foresaw we would do by our own power.

Many Catholic theologians were horrified by what Molina invented and labeled it as nothing more than a modern twist on the old Pelagian heresy. They almost succeeded in getting one Pope to condemn it as heresy.

But opposition to Molinism died down once it was seen that it deceived ignorant Protestants quite easily. Jesuit universities in Protestant countries made a point of indoctrinating Molinism into those Protestants who foolishly chose to be educated by them.

As these Jesuit-trained Protestants rose to prominence in Evangelical circles, they in turn introduced the Jesuit doctrine of Molinism in Protestant circles. But knowing that the average Protestant was suspicious of anything coming from the bloodthirsty Jesuits who had murdered their forefathers, it was decided to rename the doctrine "Middle Knowledge" instead of "Molinism" in an attempt to hide its

Jesuit origins. But a rose by any other name still smells the same.

A few Protestant supporters of Molinism such as William Lane Craig have admitted the Jesuit origin of the doctrine and even warned that Molina had defective views of grace.[25] His honesty and openness on such issues is commendable. But the vast majority of those who teach it either ignorantly or deceptively hide its historical origins.

HOW TO UNDERCUT THE GOSPEL

Molina saw that the best way to undercut the gospel was to deny that we are spiritually incapable of pleasing God. Instead, he put forth the old Greek humanist idea that man is totally and absolutely free from the effects of Adam's Fall into sin and guilt. Man's "free will" is thus not in bondage to sin and the freedom of the will remains unimpaired. Molina emphasized the *unrestrained* freedom of the will.

We once again are confronted with an *apriori* commitment to a pagan worldview in which man is autonomous. We searched in vain for any substantial exegetical evidence put forth by Molina to *prove* that man is autonomous. He merely assumes that this is true and proceeds from there.

THE FATAL ERROR

This is the fatal error with all those who follow Molina. Such Christian humanistic philosophers as Alvin

---

[25] William Lane Craig, *The Only Wise God* (Grand Rapids, Mich.; Baker, 1987).

Plantinga[26] and William Lane Craig,[27] Frank Beckwith[28] and those who follow them, naively assume the pagan doctrine of human autonomy as their starting point. They *assume* that if God predetermines the future, then man is not responsible.[29]

A WORD OF CLARIFICATION

We must stop for a moment and emphasize that when we point out that some philosopher or theologian within Christian circles is a humanistic thinker and is teaching a pagan worldview, this does not mean that we are judging his heart. A man can be a Christian in his heart, a good father, kiss babies, pet dogs, etc., but be a pagan in his worldview at the same time. Being saved is no guarantee that you do not have pagan ideas floating around in your head. We are using Scripture to judge if a man's philosophy or theology is humanistic. We have no interest in judging people's hearts. God will do that on the Day of Judgment (1 Cor. 4:1-5).

---

[26] Alvin C. Plantinga, *God, Freedom, and Evil* (Grand Rapids, Mich.; Eerdmans, 1974).

[27] William Lane Craig, *The Only Wise God* , ibid. See also his chapter in Pinnock's book, *The Grace of God, The Will of Man* (Grand Rapids, Mich.; Zondervan, 1989) and several chapters in Nash's book, *On Process Theology*.

[28] Frank Beckwith and Stephen Parrish, *The Mormon Concept of God.* (Lewiston: Wales:1991).

[29] Some faculty members at Talbot, Biola, Trinity International University and Law School, Simon Greenleaf, and other apologetic ministries in Southern California have fallen into the false teachings of Molinism. This is a serious situation that has grave implications for their ultimate view of the inspiration of the Bible and the atonement.

A Word of Warning

When you begin to refute such humanistic doctrines as Middle Knowledge, be prepared for those who support it to attack your *character* instead of answering your arguments. They will slander you behind your back saying that you are mean, unloving, unkind, a racist, prejudiced and intolerant. They will even try to stop you from speaking. Why? They fear the Light! The last thing they want is to let people know that the Bible is against their doctrines.

Problems With Middle Knowledge

The problems with the doctrine of "Middle Knowledge" are so profound and extensive that the committed Christian who loves the Lord and obeys Scripture can have nothing to do with it. This is why those who follow it will often attack your motives and character. Thankfully, there are rare exceptions where false doctrine and kind manners come together in the same person. We have never understood why people can't disagree without being disagreeable.

Not a Biblical or Apostolic Doctrine

The first problem that the supporters of Middle Knowledge face is that it is not a part of apostolic and historic Christianity. In Jude 3, we are told:

> …to continue your vigorous defense of *the faith that was passed down to the saints once and for all.*
>
> ἔσχον γράψαι ὑμῖν παρακαλῶν ἐπαγωνίζεσθαι τῇ ἅπαξ παραδοθείσῃ τοῖς ἁγίοις πίστει.

Biblical theologians have always believed and taught that if a doctrine is *new*, then it is *not* true. If it is true, then it will not be new. The Reformers spent a great deal of time and energy tracing their doctrines in church history all the way back to the first century. Why did they do this? They had two reasons that weighed heavily on their mind.

First, from Jude 3, it is obvious that "the Faith;" i.e., the body of doctrines that constitutes biblical Christianity, was delivered once and for all of time in the first century in the teachings of Jesus and the Apostles (Eph. 2:20; 3:4-5). The Christian Church is to defend the doctrines given by the Apostles (Acts 2:42). If the Apostles did not teach a doctrine, it does not constitute a part of "the Faith."

Second, Jude used the aroist tense when he used the word παραδοθείσῃ (delivered) to emphasize the finality of the Faith. When it comes to doctrine or morals, there will be no "new" revelations after the New Testament. The principle of *sola scriptura* means that what we believe and how we live are to be determined by Scripture *alone.*

This understanding works well when we deal with the Book of Mormon, the Divine Principle or the visions of Ellen White. They cannot be accepted because they teach new doctrines that were not a part of biblical and historic Christianity.

It is a wonder to us that some of those involved in the Middle Knowledge doctrine will refute Mormonism by pointing out the recent origins of Smith's doctrine and then turn around and say that the fact that the doctrine of Middle Knowledge is of recent origin has no bearing on the issue! Hypocrisy has no limits!

What should we do with doctrines such as Middle Knowledge that have appeared only in recent church history?

All the Protestant and Roman Catholic reference works that deal with the history and origin of the doctrine of Middle Knowledge state that it was invented by a Jesuit priest by the name of Luis de Molina as part of the counter-Reformation.

IN PRINCIPLE NOT IN SCRIPTURE

Since Molinism (or Middle Knowledge) is clearly of recent origin, it is not a part of "the Faith once for all delivered to the saints." *Thus it cannot in principle be found in Scripture because the authors of the Bible died many centuries before Molina invented the doctrine.* How then can some of those who teach the false doctrine of Molinism claim to find it in the Bible? By reading it back into biblical texts and thereby committing the hermenutical fallacy of eisegesis.

Most of those who teach this Jesuit doctrine will usually give "rational" arguments instead of doing any hard exegesis. Being humanists in their thinking, they assume that whatever they can come up with by "thinking" about it, has to be true. Thus, they will talk endlessly about someone doing this or that in the future. There is no need to bring a Bible to their lectures. Frank Beckwith is a good example of this procedure.[30]

FRANK BECKWITH'S PROOFS FOR MIDDLE KNOWLEDGE

In his discussion of the Omniscience of God in his book, *The Mormon Concept of God*, how does Beckwith *prove* that the Jesuit doctrine of Middle Knowledge is true?

First, he uses two illustrations: Pat mowing the lawn on Tuesday and Jim marrying Kim. That's it! He does *not* bring up a single Scripture. Why? As all humanistic thinkers, he assumes that *he* is autonomous. Thus *he* can come up with

[30] *Mormon Concept of God*, ibid. ppg. 12-13.

the truth *without* special revelation from God. He assumes that if he can think of this or that hypothetical situation, which seems to *his* mind to prove Middle Knowledge, then it is automatically true.

What Beckwith and other Molinists fail to understand is that while stories and illustrations may clarify a doctrine, they can never establish its truthfulness. They are great at spinning stories and illustrations by the dozens. But until they come up with solid exegetical evidence for their position, we are not interested. Speculative theology has always ended in heresy.

Second, while Beckwith never quoted from Scripture, he did quote the "guru of Evangelical Middle Knowledge," Dr. William Lane Craig. But Craig's citation does not contain any Scripture either. But that does not bother Beckwith or many others because, to some of them, Craig's words are just as authoratative as Scripture.

QUESTIONS FOR MOLINISTS

- Are God's decisions or decrees in eternity determined by what He sees will happen in the future?
- Thus, is God's foreknowledge prior to and hence the origin of God's decrees?
- Or, is what will happen in the future determined by what God decided or decreed in eternity?
- Thus, are God's decrees prior to His foreknowledge; i.e., is what He foresees what He has decreed shall happen?
- Did God decree to create the universe because He first saw that it would be created?

- Or was the universe created because God decreed it?
- Which came first, the decree to create or the divine foreknowledge of creation?
- Did the future universe limit God's knowledge?
- Is God's knowledge dependent or independent of the future universe?
- Is His knowledge derived or deduced?
- Is time the same for God as it is for us?
- Does God "look into the future" like a man looking through a telescope?
- Does God really have "foreknowledge" or is that word anthropomorphic?
- Does God control the future or does the future control God?
- Is the past, present and future the same for God as it is for man?
- Is God's will determined by what man will do?
- Or does God's will determine what man will do?
- Is God free?
- What kind of freedom does He have?
- Is He free to sin, to lie, to fail, etc.?
- Is God's will limited by His nature, thus He cannot sin?
- Can man interfere with God's free will?

- Does man's "free will" triumph over God's free will?
- Or shall God's will be done on earth as it is in heaven?
- Is it "My will be done" or "Thy will be done"?
- In the finite universe God created for His glory, how many ultimate free wills can there be?
- Does man have a "free will"?
- Does the Bible ever discuss the subject of man's free will?
- Can you give even one passage where this is done?
- Is man free to be perfect and sinless?
- Can you choose to be sinless today?
- If not, why not?
- Is man free to be omnipotent and omniscient?
- Can God ever interfere with man's free will?
- Does the decree of inspiration follow foreknowledge; i.e., did God will to inspire the book of Romans (or any other Scripture) because He first saw Paul writing it?
- Did the authors of the Bible write their books because God willed it or did He will it because He saw them writing them?
- Is man's free will perfect and infallible?
- Or is it imperfect and fallible?

- If man's free will is imperfect and fallible, then how can the Bible be perfect and infallible?
- If God cannot interfere with man's free will, what prevented Paul or any other author of the Bible from putting mistaken ideas and contradictory information in it?
- Did God violate the free wills of the authors of Scripture and allow them to write only what He wanted them to write?
- Did God will that Christ would die because He first saw that He would die?
- Or did Christ die because God willed it?
- Was the betrayal and execution of Christ necessary?
- Did all the events and choices of the men involved in the atonement have to happen the way they happened?
- Could Judas have decided at the last moment not to betray Jesus and thus abort the atonement?
- Was Herod or Pilot free to let Jesus go and prevent the atonement?
- What prevented some soldier from breaking the bones of Christ?
- Was it just lucky that no one broke His bones?
- Were the death of Christ and all the choices and acts of the men that made it transpire a part of God's eternal predetermined plan for history?

- Did they do what they did because God planned it?
- Was the death of Christ a fluke or an accident that was not in God's plans?
- Was the atonement something God decided to do in order to make something good come out of the death of Christ, which He foresaw would happen but did not ordain to happen?
- Was Peter certainly going to deny the Lord three times or was it possible for him not to do it even though Christ predicted it?
- Has God fixed, appointed, predestined or ordained the times and seasons?
- In prophecy, is God telling us what He definitely knows will happen in the future?
- Or, is there an element of chance or luck concerning the future that means that it does not necessarily have to come true?
- Does God love us because He first saw us loving Him?
- Does God choose us because He first saw us choosing Him?
- Did God will to give us grace because He first saw us repenting and believing?

- Which is right?

As many as were ordained to eternal life believed.
As many as believed were ordained to eternal life.

You did not choose Me but I chose you.
I chose you because you first chose Me.

If the Lord wills, we will go to a city and make a profit.
If we go to a city and make a profit, then the Lord wills it.

I will come to Rome, if God wills it.
If I go to Rome, then God wills it.

Man proposes but God disposes.
God proposes but man disposes.

God works in man the willing and the doing
Man works in God the willing and the doing.

God's will determines the casting of the lots.
The casting of the lots determines God's will.

- Where in the Bible is human autonomy clearly taught?

- Is the "freedom" spoken of in Scripture a moral work of Christ in which He sets us free from the penalty, power and presence of sin?
- Where in the Bible is the absolute freedom of human autonomy discussed or taught?
- Is salvation a reward for what God sees we will do in the future?
- Is damnation a punishment for what God sees we will do in the future?
- Does man have "natural powers" to repent and believe?
- After the Fall, was man's will affected by sin? In what ways?
- Can we please God by our own natural powers?
- Can the saints in heaven sin?
- If not, are they free?
- In the eternal state, is there a chance that someone will sin and start the whole mess over again?
- Should we begin with God or man in our worldview?
- In your worldview, is it possible for Christ to die all over again?
- Do you believe that the future is open to chance and luck?
- Does the future hold infinite possibilities?
- Was the time/space universe created as one?

- Can we separate time from space?
- Do you believe that time is eternal but space created?
- If time is eternal, is God eternally "in" time or is time eternally "in" God?
- Is God therefore dependent upon time for His existence?
- If God is dependent upon time for His existence, is time the true GOD above God?
- What about the heathen?
- Are there any valid excuses the heathen can give God as to why He cannot throw them into hell?

CONCLUSION

In this brief study of the nature and extent of God's knowledge, we have demonstrated that the historic Christian view is in line with the clear teaching of Scripture. God knows *all* things including the *future.* His foreknowledge is certain and infallible because it flows from His eternal decrees. The Bible describes the wicked as the only ones who deny or limit God's knowledge.

Today, it is necessary to warn God's people that false teachers have arisen who will deny "the faith oncc for all of time delivered to the saints." But we must follow the Apostle Paul who said,

> Let God be true even if this makes everyone a liar (Rom. 3:4).
>
> μὴ γένοιτο· γινέσθω δὲ ὁ θεὸς ἀληθής, πᾶς δὲ ἄνθρωπος ψεύστης,

RESOURCES

In a future book on Molinism, we will demonstrate in detail that the doctrine of Middle Knowledge undercuts the inspiration and inerrancy of Scripture, the substitutionay atonement of Christ and Divine Providence. It is part of the humanistic "slippery slope" that, once you start down it, will land you in atheism.

The philosophical and theological problems with Molinism are discussed at great length in Dr. Robert McGregor Wright's book, *No Place for Sovereignty*, and in the collection of essays in *The Grace of God and the Bondage of the Will*, ed. Thomas Schreiner and Bruce Ware. We recommend these works as the place to begin.

For those who wish to investigate the subject of God's knowledge in greater depth, the following works are helpful.

BOOKS WHICH PROMOTE THE BIBLICAL VIEW OF GOD AND MAN AND REFUTE PROCESS THEOLOGY AND MIDDLE KNOWLEDGE

Gleason Archer, *Encyclopedia of Bible Difficulties* (Grand Rapids, Mich.; Zondervan, 1982). See ppg 80-81, 173-174.

Baker's Dictionary of Theology (Grand Rapids, Mich.; Baker, 1960). See ppg 225, 229-230, 241.

David Banister and Random Banister, eds., *Predestination and Freewill* (Downers Grove, IL: InterVarsity, 1986). The chapters by John Feinberg and Norman Geisler.

William Bates, *The Harmony of the Divine Attributes in the Contrivance and Accomplishment of Man's Redemption* (Harrisonburg, VA.; Sprinkle Pub. 1985).

Louis Berkhof, *Systematic Theology* (Edinburgh: Banner of Truth, 1977). See ppg 66-69.

G. C. Berkouwer, *Man: The Image of God* (Grand Rapids, Mich.; Eerdmans, 1962). See chapter nine.

Harry Buis, *Historic Protestantism and Predestination* (Grand Rapids, Mich.; Baker, 1958).

The Catholic Encyclopedia (Nashville, TN; Nelson, 1987) See p. 396.

D. A. Carson, *Divine Sovereignty and Human Responsibility* (Atlanta, GA; John Knox, 1981).

Gordon Clark, *Religion, Reason and Revelation* (Nutley, NJ; Craig Press, 1961).

Cyclopedia of Biblical, Theological and Ecclesiastical Literature, (Grand Rapids, Mich.; Baker, 1981) See vol. VI. ppg 440-441.

Robert L. Dabney, *Lectures In Systematic Theology* (Grand Rapids, Mich.; Zondervan, 1972). See ppg 154-164.

The Works of Jonathan Edwards (Edinburgh: Banner of Truth, 1974). See vol. I, *A Careful and Strict Inquiry Into the Modern Prevailing Notions of the Freedom of Will,* particularly Part II, Sections XI-XIII.

The Encyclopedia of Philosophy, ed. Paul Edwards, (NY:Macmillan, 1987). See: vol. 7, ppg 338-339.

Royce Gruenler, *The Inexhaustible God* (Grand Rapids, Mich.; Baker, 1983).

The Grace of God and The Bondage of the Will, eds. Thomas Schreiner and Bruce Ware (Grand Rapids, Mich.; Baker, 1995). See vol. 2, ppg 429-497 for a detailed refutation of Middle Knowledge.

James Hastings, *Encyclopedia of Religion and Ethics* (Edinburgh: T & T Clark, 1926).

Carl F. Henry, *God, Revelation and Authority* (Waco, TX: Word: 1976). See vols. V and VI where he refutes process theology and Middle Knowledge.

Charles Hodge, *Systematic Theology* (London: James Clarke, 1960). See vol. I, ppg 398-401.

Robert A. Morey, *Battle of the Gods* (Southbridge, MA: Crowne, 1989).

Robert A. Morey, *Death and the Afterlife* (Minn:Bethany House, 1982).

Robert A. Morey, *Studies In the Atonement* (Faith Defenders, Orange, CA., 92863; 1989).

Ronald Nash, *The Concept of God* (Grand Rapids, Mich.; Zondervan, 1983). See pgs. 62-66.

John Piper, *The Justification of God* (Grand Rapids, Mich.; Baker, 1983).

On Process Theology (Grand Rapids, Mich.; Baker, 1988) See the chapters by Nash, Gruenler, Henry, Bloesch, Demarest, Peterson, Holmes, Craig, Clarke, and Morris.

N. L. Rice, *God Sovereign and Man Free: Or the Doctrine of Divine Foreordination and Man's Free Agency, Stated, Illustrated, and Proved from the Scriptures.* (Harrisonburg, VA: Sprinkle Pub., 1985).

Francis Schaeffer, *How Should We Then Live?* (Old Tappan, NJ: Fleming Revell, 1976).

Francis Schaeffer, *The God Who Is There* (Downers Grove, IL: InterVarsity, 1968).

Schaff-Herzog, *Encyclopedia of Religious Knowledge* (NY: Funk & Wagnalls, 1891). See vol. I, p 532-533, the article "Congregatio De Auxilis Divine Gratiae" and vol. III, p. 1546 the article under "Molina."

Augustus Strong, *Systematic Theology* (Valley Forge, PA:Judson Press, 1976).

Francis Turrentin, Institutes of Elenctic Theology (Harmony, NJ: P & R, 1992), I:212-220.

Robert K. McGregor Wright, *No Place for Sovereignty: What's Wrong With Freewill Theism* (Downers Grove IL; InterVarsity, 1996).

BOOKS WHICH PROMOTE THE DOCTRINE OF HUMAN AUTONOMY

David Basinger and Randall Basinger, eds., *Predestination and Freewill* (Downers Grove, IL; InterVaristy, 1986). The chapters by Bruce Reichenbach and Clark Pinnock.

Frank Beckwith, *The Mormon Concept of God* (Lewiston, NY: Edwin Mellen, 1991). See ppg 11-13.

Gregory Boyd, *Cynic Sage or Son of God* (Grand Rapids, Mich.; Baker, 1995).

Gregory Boyd, *God at War* (Downers Grove, IL: InterVarsity, 1997).

Gregory Boyd, *Jesus Under Siege* (Colorodo Springs, CO: Victor Books, 1995).

Gregory Boyd, *Letters From a Skeptic* (Colorodo Springs, CO: Chariot Victor Books, 1994).

Gregory Boyd, *Trinity In Process* (New York NY; Peter Lang, 1992).

William Lane Craig, *The Only Wise God* (Grand Rapids, Mich.; Baker, 1987). See also his chapter in Pinnock's book, *The Grace of God, The Will of Man* (Grand Rapids, Mich.; Zondervan, 1989) and several chapters in Nash's book, *On Process Theology.*

Stephen Davis, *Logic and the Nature of God* (Grand Rapids, Mich.; Eerdmans, 1983).

The Grace of God, the Will of Man, ed. Clark Pinnock, (Grand Rapids, Mich.; Zondervan, 1989).

Roy Elseth, *Did God Know?* (St. Paul, Minn: Calvary United Church, 1977). See ppg 97, 123-125. He argues that history is *not* the unfolding of God's plan; that prophecy can fail; that God had nothing to do with the death of Christ. God's plan, according to him, did not have Jesus dying on the cross!

Luis de Molina, *On Divine Foreknowledge* (Ithaca, NY: Cornell University, 1988).

George Otis, Jr., Sharing Your Faith (Chicago: Bible Research Fellowship, 1976).

George Otis, Jr., "The Foreknowledge of God," unpublished paper, 1941.

Alvin Plantinga, *God, Freedom and Evil* (Grand Rapids, Mich.; Baker, 1974).

Richard Rice, *The Openness of God* (Nashville TN; Review and Herald, 1979). Later reprinted by Bethany House in 1985 under the title, *God's Foreknowledge and*

Man's Free Will. The Bethany House edition dropped the section on Ellen G. White knowing the future. Rice argues that God did not know that Christ would die.

INDEX

AUTHORS CITED

REFERENCE WORKS CITED

SCRIPTURES CITED

About the Author

Christian Scholars Press has made the conscious decision to accept the hard challenges, the difficult questions fired at biblical scholars and the subtle mis-conceptions which creep into the community of believers.

- Some challenges are inherent in the text; some are designed to unsettle our faith.
- Some questions arise legitimately from the Scripture and are answered by our growing understanding of it; some are fired like cannonballs against the teaching of Scripture.
- Some mis-conceptions exist as we develop our knowledge and our thinking in search of the ground zero of biblical truth; some are traps covertly placed in our path in order to lead us into convenient error.

Dr. Morey is uniquely qualified to assist us in discerning the differences and defining the truth of God as taught in Scripture. His expertise in the original languages and his well-trained mind give him unique ability to lead us in these inquiries, and to find solid answers from the Word of God.

Around him, Dr. Morey has gathered a group of dedicated workers whose hearts and talents are dedicated to preserving studies like "The Nature and Extent of God's Knoweldge" and presenting them to the public in many forms – radio, TV, printed matter and every electronic means.

Your time will be well spent as you delve into the great questions of our day under the guidance of Dr. Robert A. Morey.

The Battle of the Gods

This book is the most detailed biblical exposition and defense of the Christian concept of God in the last century. Some scholars have said that it is the greatest work on the attributes of God since Charnock! It refutes the "Open View of God" that is being taught in many circles.

"Today, God's character and attributes are again being called into question. Some well-known theologians have resurrected neo-pagan views of God and have tried to pass them off as Christian. Dr. Morey has written the definitive rebuttal to the 'God as finite' view. May God use it to arrest this abomination before it spreads."
—Dr. D. James Kennedy, Coral Ridge Ministries

"In addressing those views which teach that God is in some way finite or limited, Morey proves unrelenting. The pagan origins and history of the 'finite God' teaching are examined and documented. The arguments for such teachings are shown to be built on flawed logic and weak foundations. In the vernacular, Morey has 'dusted off the spot' on which any teachings that God is limited may be able to stand." **—John Ankerberg, TV & Radio Talk Show Host**

The general Christian public is not yet aware that pagan ideas about God continue to infiltrate the Evangelical community. Men respected as Evangelical scholars, such men as Richard Rice and Clark Pinnock, are accused of embracing dangerous aspects of process theology. Morey cites convincing evidence for his accusation. Morey has built an excellent base for his contention—rejection of a totally inerrant Bible inevitably results in man instead of God becoming the measure.—**Dr. Robert P. Lightner, Dallas Seminary**

To order, send check or money order in the amount of $19.95 plus $6.00 (S&H):

Faith Defenders

P. O. Box 7447, Orange CA 92863

Or call: 1(800) 41-TRUTH

Or go on line at: www.faithdefenders.com